BIRMINGHAM

in the age of the tram

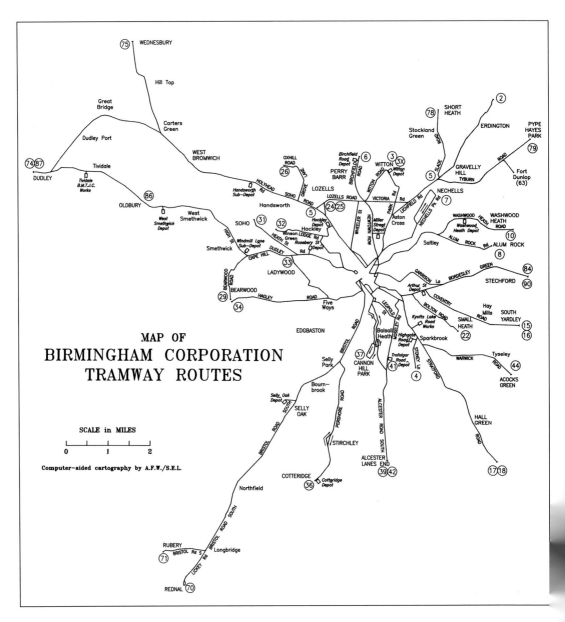

MAP OF
BIRMINGHAM CORPORATION
TRAMWAY ROUTES

SCALE in MILES

0   1   2

Computer–aided cartography by A.F.W./S.E.L.

Map of Birmingham Corporation tramway routes. This map shows the whole of the Birmingham tramway network, including Nechells, Bolton Road, and routes along Bristol Road to Rubery and Rednal, along Pershore Road to Cotteridge, and through Balsall Heath and along Moseley Road to Alcester Lanes End. It does not purport to show the system at any given date, being intended to locate each route to scale and place it in its geographical location. Only the route numbers of regular all-day tramcar services are shown. For detail of trackwork and locations of short working turning points, see the definitive maps by J. C. Gillham, extracts of which are given in each chapter.

BIRMINGHAM

in the age of the tram
1933-53

The south-western routes

Bristol Road routes to Rubery and Rednal,
Pershore Road to Cotteridge,
Balsall Heath and Moseley Road routes
to Alcester Lanes End,
plus Nechells and Bolton Road

David Harvey

·THE NOSTALGIA OF BRITAIN·
from
The NOSTALGIA Collection

First published in 1994 as *A Nostalgic Look at Birmingham Trams 1933-1953 Volume 2*
Adapted and republished in this format 2004

British Library Cataloguing in Publication Data
A catalogue record for this book is available from the British Library.
ISBN 1 85794 182 9

Silver Link Publishing Ltd
The Trundle
Ringstead Road
Great Addington
Kettering
Northants NN14 4BW

Tel/Fax: 01536 330588
email: sales@nostalgiacollection.com
Website:
www.nostalgiacollection.com

Printed and bound in Great Britain

A Silver Link book
from
The NOSTALGIA *Collection*

ACKNOWLEDGEMENTS

The original book upon which this new edition is based would not have been possible without all those tram enthusiasts and photographers whose work is credited within the main text.

I am extremely grateful to R. Brook, the late W. A. Camwell, John Edgington, F. N. Lloyd Jones, the late L. W. Perkins, K. Terry, C. C. Thornburn, the late J. S. Webb, the late Ray Wilson, and the late W. J. Wyse for allowing me access to their photographic collections and providing me with information and dates about their photographs. In particular, the contribution of Peter Jaques towards this volume was invaluable.

I am extremely grateful to the late John Stanford for all his valuable comments about dates, advertisements and individual tramcar details, and to Richard Weaver for commenting upon and editing the original manuscript. To the late Norman Glover, whose photographs appear in this volume, I extend special thanks a his personal recollections of Birmingham tram provide a fascinating insight into the system o over 40 years ago; he also took great care ove the editing of the final draft of the text.

My thanks also go to John Gillham fo allowing me to use extracts from hi Birmingham track layout maps, and to Stan Letts and Arthur Whitehouse for producing the general layout map of the Birmingham tram system. It is with great sadness that thank Doug Clayton for allowing me to use hi Dufay colour photograph of car 842, whic appears on the front cover and was borrowe from him in 2004. Unfortunately he die before the book was published so never sav his unique photograph in print.

Finally, as before, I must thank my wife Diana; her critical comments, encouragemen and patience made this volume's productio considerably easier.

CONTENTS

In September 1949, only days before the closure of the Moseley Road group of tram services, tired-looking tramcar 420 stops at the compulsory stop outside Digbeth Civic Hall, and a passenger ambles out in front of the Daimler COG5 double-decker. The CVP-registered bus is working on the newly introduced 54 service to Stuarts Rd, Stechford, which had only been running since the 84 tram route was abandoned on 2 October 1948; the same fate would soon befall the Moseley Road tram routes. Car 420 is a UEC open-balcony 40hp four-wheeler of 1912, one of the last four-wheelers bought by the Corporation; all 50 were fitted with the Spencer-Dawson air and oil brake soon after they entered service so that they could work the 1 in 13 hill in Leopold Street. Once loaded, the tram will immediately turn right, across the recently abandoned Stechford tram tracks, into Rea Street, where Midland Red's Digbeth garage was located. The waste ground fronting Digbeth on the corner of Rea Street had been cleared, but because of the war was not developed until Spencer House and the Digbeth Coach Station were opened on it in 1958. Meanwhile it was used by Midland Red as a parking overspill area for the garage, and behind the Belisha beacon can be seen the mesh fencing around it. Parked there are a wartime Weymann-bodied Guy 'Arab' II and a late pre-war SOS FEDD with a brush body. *A. N. Porter*

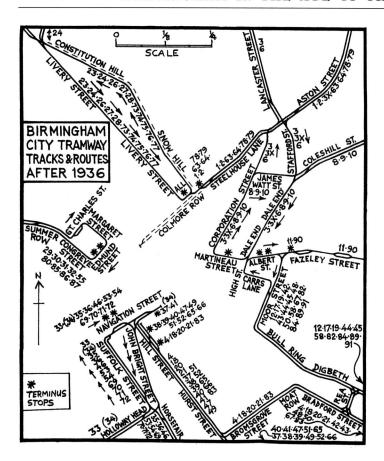

Left Birmingham City tramway tracks and routes after 1936. It can be seen that the city centre was never directly crossed by any route. This meant that tramcars transferring to another depot or going to Kyotts Lake Works frequently had to make circuitous journeys through the back streets around the perimeter of the city centre.

Termini in Birmingham city centre of the routes covered by this book.
A: Edmund Street (31, 32); E: Steelhouse Lane (1, 2, 63, 64, 78, 79); F: Martineau Street (3, 3X, 6, 7, 8, 9, 10); G: Dale End to Albert Street (13, 15, 17, 19, 44, 45, 56, 58, 82, 89, 91); K: Station Street (14, 16, 57); L: Station Street to Hill Street (18, 20, 21, 83); Q: Navigation Street (33, 34)

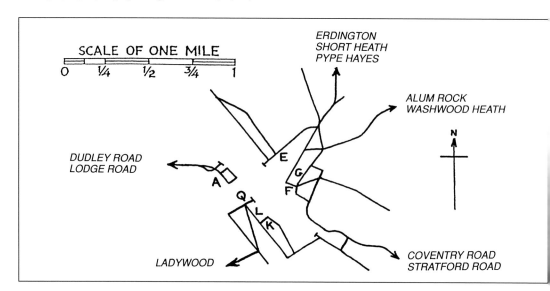

INTRODUCTION

The Birmingham tram system was the fourth largest in Britain after London, Glasgow and Manchester, but to many tramway enthusiasts its tall, gaunt, dark blue and primrose tramcars all tended to look the same as each other. Yet, in a fleet totalling 843 cars owned by Birmingham Corporation, there were variations, modifications and differences among the 489 four-wheelers and the 354 eight-wheeled bogie tramcars. Although most depots had a selection of trams from a number of different types, there was a tendency for particular classes of tram to be associated with a group of routes at a specific point in time. Thus, in terms of this book the Cotteridge route was always linked to the 812 Class and the two lightweight trams, 842 and 843, while Moseley Road depot's 401 Class of open-balconied four-wheelers were rarely to be found anywhere else.

Like the other books in this series, this one shows the Second City's trams and their routes in a geographical, historical and social context. The streets of Birmingham that resounded to the rumblings of the trams have been largely altered out of all recognition. Redevelopment of the central area, either to replace time-expired buildings or to relieve congestion, swept away many landmarks such as Snow Hill Station, the subterranean toilets at the Dale End-Bull Street junction and Kunzle's cake shop in Martineau Street.

In the inner suburbs, where the tramcar had reigned supreme as the transport for the 'working man', wartime bombing cut great swathes through the Victorian terraces and the town planners were poised to sweep away some 30,000 sub-standard back-to back properties. Housing in the city from the late 1930s was in a desperate plight; there were still 6,500 houses without a separate water supply, 81,500 without a bath and, as late as 1947, just over 400 properties without gas or electricity.

The inner areas of Ladywood, Newtown, Nechells, Highgate and Lee Bank were the first areas to be redeveloped and, in most cases, the passing of the tramcar was the prelude to a change in what had been a stable, if deteriorating, urban landscape – change that was to eradicate totally a way of life in the city. The mixture of houses and factories in areas such as Saltley, Duddeston and Aston disappeared, taking away whole communities from their dingy, treeless environments to the new estates being constructed either locally or at the edge of the city.

By the time that this redevelopment was starting, the trams had largely gone, and the more flexible bus was the prime mover of the population. When the trams finally were abandoned in the city, Birmingham had the dubious distinction of being the largest city in the world not to have any form of electric transport.

This book looks at basically the southern routes of the city, from about 1933, although earlier views are included. The routes covered in detail are the Bristol Road services, the Cotteridge route, the Moseley Road and Alcester Lanes End tram routes, and the complex route network in the Balsall Heath area. As in the companion volumes, each route is covered by a pictorial survey, using where possible previously unpublished photographs, from the city centre to the outer terminus.

Two early abandonments are also covered in the volume: the first and second tram routes to be abandoned in the city were Nechells (1922) and Bolton Road (1930). These routes are not in the southern area of the city but are included here so that overall, in this series of books, the complete Birmingham system of tram routes, including those abandoned prior to 1933, can be covered.

The Nechells route

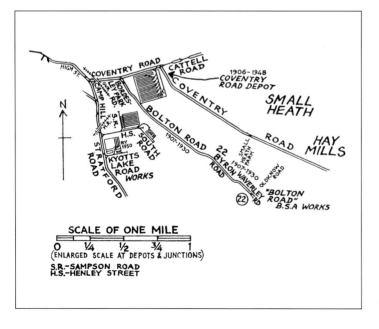

The Bolton Road route

EARLY ABANDONMENTS

Nechells

The Nechells route was opened on 1 January 1907 to replace the last City of Birmingham Tramway Company (CBT) horse-tram route in the city. This had its terminus at the bottom of Albert Street and had gone via Curzon Street, Vauxhall Road and Bloomsbury Street before gaining the steep descent past the stables and depot in Long Acre.

The replacement electric tram service, which in 1915 was numbered 7, had its city terminus at the top of Martineau Street, and was usually operated by four-wheel Radial cars from Washwood Heath depot. The route followed the Perry Barr trams along Corporation Street, but then went into Aston Street as far as Gosta Green. The trams left this former medieval open space and passed into Lister Street, crossing Holt Street, with its brewery, before launching themselves over the humped-back bridge that carried Lister Street over the Birmingham & Fazeley Canal and on towards the distant Nechells gas works. At the bottom of the bridge was the important factory-lined Dartmouth Street, and beyond the mixture of houses and small workshops that lined Great Lister Street. The route continued towards Saltley for about half a mile until it arrived at Bloomsbury Street, just before Saltley Road, where it would have met the Washwood Heath and Alum Rock tram routes. It then turned left into Bloomsbury Street, regaining the former horse-tram route.

The route climbed gently to the north-east until Nechells Green was reached at the corner of Nechells Place. From here the route began

An unidentified, open-vestibuled, four-wheel Radial tram of the 71-220 Class climbs Nechells Park Road near Stanley Road, on the inward leg of its loop around Nechells. This car's fleet number cannot be identified clearly but it has only two digits and is therefore numbered in the 80 or 90 series. It is carrying the pre-1915 flop-over destination boards at the front of the open balcony. Just below it, on the dash panel, the tram is advertising the Empire Theatre, which was on the corner of Smallbrook Street and Hurst Street. The CBT horse-tram service had its city terminus in Albert Street and was the last horse-tram service to operate in Birmingham. It used ten specially constructed knife-board double-deckers that were kept in a depot off Nechells Park Road in nearby Butlin Street. The route was finally abandoned on 26 November 1922, and without ceremony trolleybuses took over, although they did not use the outer one-way leg along the parallel Long Acre.

The boy with the hoop stands at the corner of Chattaway Street in front of the steeply descending terraced housing, of a slightly superior nature with wrought-iron fencing and their small downstairs bay-windows. With the young lady dressed in the shorter skirt and the older woman in the more conservatively styled long skirt, this view dates from about 1910. *Commercial postcard*

Photographs of anything 'tramwise' working on the Nechells service 7 are extremely rare, yet one of the most common commercial postcards was taken at Nechells Green on 7 July 1909 on the occasion of the Royal visit to Birmingham, when King Edward VII and Queen Alexandra opened the University of Birmingham's new campus in Edgbaston. Open-top Brill truck car 266 was withdrawn from service in December 1908 and equipped with 4,000 lamps, which, combined with the legend 'Welcome To Our King & Queen', must have been an electrifying, or at least impressive, sight as it toured the city. It is in Nechells Green and is being followed by a 71 Class top-covered tram working on the short-lived Nechells to Small Heath through service. *Commercial postcard*

to run on a clockwise one-and-a-half-mile loop around Thimble Mill Lane and Long Acre to Cuckoo Road where the terminus was situated, then back up Nechells Park Road's hill and through the area's principal shopping centre before returning to Nechells Green.

The area had been developed in the 1840s with back-to-back houses mixed in with the later bye-laws terraces of the 1860s and 1870s. Some slightly more prosperous houses had been built at the northern end of Nechells Park Road, but the area around Cuckoo Road, sandwiched between the Tame valley, with its sewage filter beds to the north, the Birmingham & Fazeley Canal, with its associated industrial development to the west, and to the east the dismal mass of Nechells power station, was not really conducive to attracting wealthy Victorians.

With the Chairman of the Tramways Committee, Alderman Harrison Barrow, keen to implement trailer operation using single-deck tramcars, the Nechells route was selected in 1916 to try out this experiment, as it had loop termini at both inner and outer ends. The experiment ended in 1918 and the route, in urgent need of new track but poorly subscribed, was finally abandoned on 26 November 1922. It was replaced the next day, becoming the first tram route in the country to be converted to trolleybus operation, using a batch of solid-tyred, Roe-bodied, top-covered Railless double-deckers.

Bolton Road

This service was one of the many that were opened on 1 January 1907 as part of the enormous expansion of the tramway network embarked upon by Birmingham Corporation Tramways Department.

Starting in Station Street, the Bolton Road service followed the route of Yardley trams out of the city by way of Dudley Street, Pershore Street, Moat Row, Bradford Street and Rea Street, before gaining Digbeth and High Street, Deritend. The urban landscape was that of markets, warehouses and shops, which gave way to the residential areas of Bolton and Byron Roads.

The tram route turned left into Coventry Road and under the Great Western Railway bridge at Bordesley. A little under 50 yards later the route crossed the Birmingham & Warwick Canal, and before the climb of Kingston Hill, towards Arthur Street depot, could be started, the route turned right into Bordesley Park Road. From here to the terminus, some 1½ miles away, the route ran to the north side of the extensive GWR sidings that lay alongside that railway's main line to London.

The trams ran through an area of late-Victorian terraces, those in Bolton Road being earlier than those in Byron Road, which was reached after the pastorally named Golden Hillock Road was crossed. The late-19th-century developers in this part of Small Heath

Right The terminus of the 22 Bolton Road route was on the Oldknow Road corner just before the BSA works. At the twin terminal lines was a crossover used to gain access to the city-bound line. Ex-CBT car 461 (formerly 201 in the CBT fleet) stands on the outbound stub, with the ubiquitous corner shop opposite the BSA factory. Known as the 'Aston' type, these trams were originally built by the Brush Company in 1904. By about 1929, when this photograph was taken, it had acquired a top cover and a vestibule. It is known to have been a Highgate Road tram in 1929, suggesting that this photograph was taken on a Sunday, for on this day Coventry Road and Highgate Road depots worked alternate journeys on the short Stoney Lane 4 and Bolton Road services from 1928 until the latter route's abandonment on Tuesday 4 February 1930. *R. T. Coxon collection*

Below UEC-bodied Brill 21E-trucked tram 46 is in almost original condition in Byron Road near the junction with Golden Hillock Road in about 1908. These small 48-seater trams, bodied by the United Electric Car Co of Preston, 130 of which were delivered to BCT between 1905 and 1908, were the backbone of the Edwardian tramcar fleet. Even if their three-windowed, open-topped, wooden-seated, unvestibuled condition seemed a little primitive, these little tramcars could go anywhere on the expanding tramway system. By 1910 this car had been fitted with the Maley track brake, becoming one of 54 'Brill-Maley' cars. Together with 59 others of the class, it was later fitted for snowplough operation, and received top covers and vestibules. Having run from Coventry Road for most of its life, car 46 then moved to Rosebery Street and later Witton, from where it was withdrawn in February 1937. *Commercial postcard*

One of the little three-side-windowed UEC open-top cars, 47, mounted on Brill 21E 6-foot-wheelbase trucks, which had entered service by June 1906, stands alongside the Bundy clock on the corner of Byron Road (on the left) and Waverley Road, about to move off to Station Street in the city centre. The actual terminus of the 22 route was at the entrance to the BSA works on the corner of Oldknow Road some 300 yards behind the camera. The tram is showing the letter 'B' on a blue background, which was replaced in 1915 by the route number 22. To the right of the tramcar, the terraced villas in Waverley Road date from the 1880s, and were highly prized residences as they overlooked Small Heath Park; the park occupied some 41 acres that had been donated to the city by the philanthropic Louisa Ryland and was opened by Jesse Collings, the Mayor of Birmingham, on 5 May 1879. During this Edwardian period the park could offer a refreshment room, tennis courts, a bowling green, a lovely wrought-iron bandstand and an impressive boating pool. *Author's collection*

evidently had a penchant for literature, as the trams turned right into Waverley Road opposite Tennyson Road. This junction was at the southern corner of Small Heath Park, the land for which had been donated by Miss L. A. Ryland and had been opened to the public in 1878. The park had been visited by Queen Victoria on 23 March 1887, the same day that she laid the foundation stone for the Victoria Law Courts in the town centre, and for a time the park was known as Victoria Park to commemorate the visit. The Coventry Road trams could be seen on the far side of the park as the route left its oasis and the large contemporary villas that skirted it and ran to the stub terminus in Waverley Road at the junction with Oldknow Road in the shadow of the BSA factory.

Under the 1915 route numbering system the Bolton Road tram route was allocated number 22, and for most of its life it was operated by small four-wheel trams from the 21 and 71 classes or ex-Company cars. The service was unremunerative because it relied only upon the BSA works traffic, the comparatively small amount of housing along the route with virtually no housing to the south side of Bolton Road, and its proximity to the Coventry Road services. It was the second tram route to close, and car 294 performed the final duties on Tuesday 4 February 1930. The service was replaced by one-man-operated Guy single-deck buses, and eventually the service became part of the circuitous 28 route on 2 October 1935.

BRISTOL ROAD ROUTES

Bristol Road, Bournbrook, Selly Oak, Northfield, Longbridge, Rednal and Rubery

On 24 July 1890 the Birmingham Central Tramways Co Ltd began a service along Bristol Road that was worked by accumulator cars. These looked very similar to the existing cable trams that were in operation on the Handsworth route. This unusual battery-powered method of transport used bogie cars 101-112, built by Falcon. Numerically they followed on from the 25 Handsworth cable cars. There were also two small four-wheeled accumulator cars built by Brown Marshall in 1893, but these only ran for a short time. The battery cars had replaced a 4ft 8½in standard gauge horse-tram system operated by the Birmingham & District Tramways Company, which had operated to the Bournbrook boundary at the Bournbrook Hotel from 1873.

The new method of transport terminated at Dawlish Road, just beyond the horse-tram terminus, where a new depot was built to accommodate the cars. The accumulator tramcars had a 48-seat capacity, which enabled them to move large numbers of passengers, but problems with maintaining and recharging the batteries, together with leakages of acid from them, meant that this type of tram was not totally successful.

After the City of Birmingham Tramways Company was set up on 29 September 1896 to take over the assets of the Birmingham Central company, the decline in the reliability of the battery accumulator trams caused CBT to approach the Birmingham Corporation Public Works Department with a view to rebuilding the Bristol Road line using a new fleet of overhead electric tramcars. These were introduced on Tuesday 14 May 1901, and the opportunity was taken to extend the line almost another half-mile south-westwards to Chapel Lane, Selly Oak. This was the first overhead electric route to be opened in Birmingham and utilised 15 small 48-seater

trams constructed by the Electric Railway & Tramway Carriage Works (ER&TCW), numbered 151-165.

When opened, the electric trams' city terminus was, like its predecessor, at a dead-end terminus in Suffolk Street. This terminus was considered to be too far away from the city centre, and on 4 February 1902 an anti-clockwise loop was brought into use. This used an inward line from Horse Fair along John Bright Street to a terminus at the west end of Navigation Street near to New Street Station. It then turned left into Suffolk Street and back to Horse Fair. It will be noticed that this is the reverse of the way that the loop is shown in Birmingham Corporation days, and was only changed to the more usually seen clockwise route when the Ladywood electric tram service was introduced on 17 October 1906. After this date the route itself remained largely unaltered until 1923, when the outer terminus was placed on the south side of Chapel Lane.

On leaving the terminus in Navigation Street over the western tunnel leading into New Street Station, the trams turned left into the busy built-up office area in John Bright Street. This road had been opened in 1881 and had swept away some of the worst slums in Birmingham in Cross Street and Gough Street; it opened up the town to the south-west and by the early years of the century had the added attraction of the Alexandra Theatre, opened in May 1901 and originally known as the Lyceum.

After passing Station Street, which had been used by the steam trams until the end of 1906, the important junction with Suffolk Street, Holloway Head and Smallbrook Street was reached. The trams headed southwards across this junction and passed into Horse Fair. The tram route had by now left the late-Victorian redevelopments of the city and passed into the much older houses that lined Horse Fair. This wide road was made available for the trading of horses in the late 18th century and became a prosperous market area. At Essex Street, the road turned to the south-west into Bristol Street. This street became important during the time of the horse-trams, which were introduced in the 1870s, and it prospered as the shopping area for the people of the Edgbaston and Balsall Heath suburbs around the St Lukes Road junction.

At the end of the shopping suburb at Belgrave Road, Bristol Road climbed sharply until Wellington Road was reached. From here until Priory Road and Pebble Mill Road, the route skirted the end of the Calthorpe Estate, which lay to the west. This straight section of Bristol Road was developed, from the late Regency period, as a high-class residential area with substantial houses in large grounds for the dignitaries and industrialists of Birmingham. Priory Road connected the affluent suburbs of Edgbaston and Moseley and crossed Bristol Road at the southern end of its Victorian residential growth. Just beyond this was the junction with Pebble Mill Road, where the Cotteridge-bound trams turned towards Pershore Road.

After 1924 this section of the Bristol Road route was re-positioned on to a central reservation. The last 600 yards of this section of reserved track from Eastern Road to Edgbaston Park Road was developed with

The Bristol Road routes

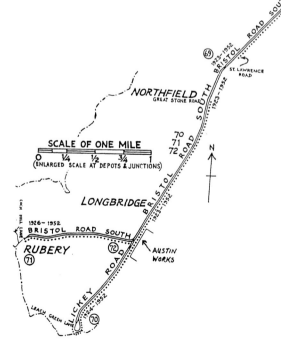

bay-windowed inter-war houses on the south-eastern side and opposite, beyond the playing fields, the school buildings of the King Edward foundation. It was along this tree-lined avenue that, after the trams were abandoned on 5 July 1952, some of the withdrawn tramcars were stored for up to three weeks before being driven away to Witton depot for scrapping.

On the hill behind the Gun Barrels public house, on the corner of Edgbaston Park Road stand the buildings of the University of Birmingham; these were begun in 1900 and opened with much civic ceremony by King Edward VII in July 1909. The University, which is actually in Edgbaston, is dominated by the Great Hall and the campanile (bell tower), both of which could be seen from a passing tramcar, some 300 yards away. The Gun Barrels public house stood virtually on the county boundary with Worcestershire and had been a centre for bare-knuckle prize fighting.

After crossing the Bourn Brook stream, the trams entered the Victorian development of Bournbrook, passing through an area that has survived virtually intact today as a suburban shopping centre. The old horse-tram stables behind the Bournbrook Hotel, renamed in the 1980s as The Old Varsity Tavern, were on the west side of Bristol Road, in Grange Road. Opposite, between Dawlish Road and Tiverton Road and still standing, was the former CBT Bournbrook accumulator and subsequent electric tramcar depot. Bournbrook depot had been built in 1891 and was to serve the Corporation's trams from its takeover of the operation of the Bristol Road routes on 1 July 1911 until the overcrowded depot was replaced by the new premises at Selly Oak.

Bristol Road then climbed a long steep incline, passing the Selly Oak Institute, built with money given by George Cadbury in 1894, before passing beneath the bridge that carried the former Midland Railway's Birmingham and West Suburban line. This line, with its later re-aligned bridge and track, and Selly Oak station just beyond the bridge on the south side of Bristol Road, had been opened initially on 3 April 1876 between the dead-end terminus at Granville Street and the Camp Hill line at Kings Norton, and had provided competition with the trams as a major carrier of commuter passengers along the Bristol Road corridor. Once the Worcester & Birmingham Canal, alongside which the Midland Railway constructed its line, was crossed, the tram route reached the top of the hill and arrived at Selly Oak, which was the third shopping area on the route. This original part of the service was numbered 35 after 1915 when route numbers were introduced.

The terminus at the Plough & Harrow public house, on the corner of Chapel Lane, also marked the position of the branch line to Selly Oak depot. This was opened with a capacity of some 80 tramcars on 12 July 1927. After 1 October 1923 the tram route was extended from Selly Oak, along further stretches of reserved track to Northfield, which was some 2½ miles away. On leaving the shopping centre at the southern end of Selly Oak, the trams crested the top of Griffins Hill at Weoley Park Road and descended the steep

hill, passing the Methodist Teachers' Colleges before reaching the wooded valley bottom at Bournville Lane and the small bridge over Griffins Brook. This area is still largely protected from urban growth as the land is owned by the Bournville Village Trust.

A further climb along the tree-lined central reservation took the tram service past the Orthopaedic Hospital and into the fourth suburban shopping centre on the route, which was the 69 route terminus. This service was developed to serve the commuter suburb that had grown as a result of the opening by the Midland Railway of its railway station at Northfield in 1869. The later Edwardian growth to the east of the main Bristol Road had gradually spread away from the medieval village centre and the need for a cheap, alternative method of transport was met by the Corporation tramcars. It was a vicious circle, as the introduction of the trams led to further urban expansion, so that the almost rural nature of the Bristol Road in the Northfield of the 1920s was soon to be eclipsed by expansion and left behind by a further tramway extension.

On 17 December 1923 the service was extended as the 72 route to Longbridge to replace the connecting bus services between Northfield and Longbridge, Rednal and Rubery. This extension had first been worked on 19 July 1913 using ten Daimler 40hp motorbuses. These were the first motorbus-operated services run by Birmingham Corporation and continued, despite the trials and tribulations of the First World War, until being eventually replaced by the tramway. The Austin Motor Works had been opened in 1905 near the junction of the Halesowen branch line on the Midland Railway's main line between Birmingham and Gloucester. After the ending of hostilities, the ribbon development of mainly bay-windowed semi-detached houses spread rapidly southwards away from Northfield down the steep Pigeon House Hill and subsumed the areas around the old cluster of houses at Tessall near the Austin factory. As with the Selly Oak to Northfield section, this stretch of track was laid on central reservation.

The route was next extended to Rednal on 14 April 1924, alongside Cofton Park to the

Hare & Hounds public house up the increasingly steep climb of Lickey Road. Although served for the previous 11 years by buses, the new 70 route enabled passengers to travel far more easily from the city terminus at Navigation Street the 8¼ miles to the open spaces of the Lickey Hills; this enabled the terminus area to be developed as a local tourist attraction. The following year, the distinctive 200-yard-long terminal loop with its large curved wrought-iron shelter was constructed. Originally the tramway along Lickey Road was built on the western side of the road, and when the second carriageway was built in 1939 this became the central reservation.

The last part of the Bristol Road group of routes to open was westwards along Bristol Road South to the gates of Rubery Hill Hospital near Cock Hill Lane. The 71 route served the Leach Green housing development that nestled beneath the 821-foot Rednal Hill to the south of the extension. This 1-mile section on reserved track was opened on Monday 8 February 1926, but, unlike the 1913 open-topped bus service, did not cross the city boundary into Rubery.

The Bristol Road route was for many years operated largely by the 301 Class of open-balconied four-wheelers, which saw sterling service and operated on the route until 1939. After this date they were superseded by bogie cars displaced by the closure of the Hockley services. Many of the 301 Class went to other depots to displace the ex-Radial 71 Class cars that were being withdrawn from the fleet. Towards the end of operation on the routes, more air-brake cars from initially the 732 Class and, after the closure of the Washwood Heath routes, the former bow-collector-fitted 762 Class were synonymous with this most impressive south-western section of Birmingham's tramway system, where the running time for a return trip was timetabled to take only 86 minutes.

The Bristol Road routes closed on Saturday 5 July 1952.

Navigation Street to Bournbrook

Below The terminus of the accumulator tramcar route to Bournbrook was in Suffolk Street at the junction with Navigation Street. The operation of battery accumulator trams along Bristol Road to Dawlish Road, Bournbrook, began on 24 July 1890 and was deemed successful, despite the necessity to recharge the banks of 12 batteries twice a day. The batteries were carried behind the rocker panels, and what look like six smaller panels in the rocker panels of the tramcar were in reality the individual doors to the batteries. Car 104 was constructed by the Falcon Company of Loughborough, which would become Brush Electrical before the century had ended, though retaining the falcon as its emblem. The bogie cars were 26ft 6in long and had a seating capacity of 24 inside and 26 outside. The Elwell-Parker-designed series-wound motors ran at 700rpm and gave a road speed of 8mph.

Behind the tramcar, in Navigation Street, are the thoroughfare's original buildings dating from its opening in 1769 when the Birmingham Canal Navigation' original canal between Birmingham and Wolverhampton, which had been surveyed and designed by the pioneering James Brindley, was nearing completion. Towering above these Georgian properties is the then recently constructed Birmingham Central Technical College, designed by Essex Nicol & Woodman and opened on 13 December 1895 by the Duke of Devonshire. Latterly known as Matthew Boulton Technical College, this elegant building was swept away in the 1960s when Suffolk Street Queensway was constructed as part of the Inner Ring Road scheme. *A Jenson*

Opposite top The Bristol Road and Cotteridge cars on their inward journey from Horse Fair travelled along Suffolk Street and descended to turn right into Navigation Street where the terminus was situated

They then turned right again into John Bright Street before leaving this ⅔-mile triangle and rejoining Horse Fair. One of the former Washwood Heath bow-collector cars, 768, a 1928 Brush car fitted with EMB air-brakes and EMB-built Burnley-type maximum traction bogies, stands in Suffolk Street at the yellow tram stop in June 1952. A solitary passenger is caught alighting before the tram slowly turns into Navigation Street. This corner was the site of an unfortunate accident in 1942 when tram 587 (see page 29) overturned after the driver accelerated down the short descent in Suffolk Street and failed to negotiate the sharp corner into Navigation Street after losing his bearings in the early-morning blackout. The small boy on the pavement looks curiously over his shoulder at Ray Wilson, who took so many interesting photographs of the Birmingham transport scene in the early post-war period.

The only building to survive today is the distant Baskerville House at the top of Suffolk Street, the building to the left of the gap in the skyline, which was the only wing completed of the neo-classical civic centre, in 1939. It was, according to its architect T. Cecil Howitt, based on the Belvedere Palace in Rome, but perhaps belongs better in the capital of a former communist country, as in certain quarters it is nicknamed 'The Kremlin'. Everything else has gone. On the left of Suffolk Street is the West End cinema, opened on 9 March 1925 with a performance of *Zeebrugge*, and closed on 18 March 1967 to make way for the inner ring road scheme. The building standing on the corner of Holliday Street was

the offices of the goods department of the former LMS Railway. This also disappeared, together with the buildings both opposite and behind the tram, with the construction of Suffolk Street Queensway and its tunnel, which starts approximately where the lone motorcyclist is riding. *R. T. Wilson*

Above right Turning into Navigation Street beneath the shadow of the terracotta-fronted, red-brick Birmingham Central Technical College is car 766, a Brush-bodied EMB air-brake car of 1928, working on the 71 from Rednal and negotiating the awkward turn mentioned above. The advertising hoardings hide the long-derelict site once occupied by the buildings seen behind accumulator car 104 opposite. The loop around Navigation Street and John Bright Street was introduced on 4 February 1902, replacing the dead-end terminus in Suffolk Street, which

the electric cars of CBT had inherited from the accumulator cars on 14 May 1901. Standing on the steep hill in front of the College is 1563 (GOE 563), a Daimler CVG6 with a 54-seat Metro-Cammell body built in 1947, which is working on the 20A service to Weoley Castle. Noticeable is the radiator destination slip-board, which was deemed necessary by the Selly Oak garage traffic office as the 20 service's proliferation of meandering route alternatives around the huge Weoley Castle Estate was beginning to confuse even the residents. Looking as though it is about to follow the tramcar into Navigation Street is an Austin Dorset that was first registered in August 1951. A slab-sided Singer SM1500 speeds out of the city centre past the boarded-up corner premises that had belonged to one Edward Francis Spicer, whose essential Victorian art of taxidermy had, even by 1952, long since gone out of fashion. *R. T. Wilson*

Below The distant Victorian buildings of Stephenson Street and the edge of the central shopping area of the city are reminders that in Birmingham many buildings have outlived the tram, which occupied only a short phase of the city's recent history and growth. Indeed, in view of the large-scale redevelopment, it is a little surprising that a number of existing city centre buildings actually pre-date the Bristol Road trams. These ran from 14 May 1901 until 30 June 1911 in City of Birmingham Tramways (CBT) ownership; from the following day until the abandonment on 5 July 1952 the route was operated by Birmingham Corporation.

Tram 739, one of the first batch of air-brake cars purchased by the Corporation, was built by Brush and is seen here turning into the terminal kerbside track in Navigation Street to pick up passengers for the long run back to Rednal on the 70 route. This 60-seater car will join the later Short Brothers-built car 818 at the rather splendid cast-iron shelters; the latter is working the 36 route to Cotteridge, and just beyond it is one of the 20 Guy Arab IIIs owned by Midland Red, fitted with powerful Meadows engines and Guy-built bodies to a Park Royal design, and working on one of the routes to Dudley or Wolverhampton. There are only six cars and one van visible in this 1951 view, including the early post-war, Warwickshire-registered Standard 8 in the foreground. *R. T. Wilson*

Bottom It is debatable whether modern-day health experts would agree with the slogan for K4 cigarettes, but in pre-war days every film star looked more alluring when smoking. The advertisement displayed between the decks of car 379 belongs to those far-off days when social attitudes towards smoking were very different from those of today. The tram is standing at the Navigation Street terminus on 7 April 1939, waiting to work the Bristol Road short-working, numbered 35, to Selly Oak, some ? miles away. It is one of the 361-400 Class that entered service in December 1911, built by the United Electric Car Co (UEC) to the same design as the 301-360 cars, except that they were 6 inches longer, at 29ft 9in, to accommodate the operation of the handbrake handle. With four others of the class, car 379 was involved in experiments with single-deck operation during the First World War, being converted in June 1917 but, unlike the other four, to a standee configuration. It was then used on the Cannon Hill 37 route, apparently with some success, but towards the end of 1918 these experiments came to an end, and Car 379 was refitted with a new top-deck cover in July 1923. The five re-converted single-deckers could always be distinguished by the lack of top-lights in the upper saloon. Within three years of this photograph, car 379 was repainted in the wartime grey livery after another period in store in Rosebery Street depot. It was eventually broken up at Kyotts Lake Road Works after the closure of the Witton routes in February 1950. Standing behind the open-balconied tram is car 748, a 1926 totally enclosed, Brush-built tram, working the 70 route to Rednal. *L. W. Perkins*

Above right Most views of Navigation Street looking away from the city centre towards Suffolk Street show lines of trams waiting to pick up passengers at the shelters before going off on their journeys to Cotteridge, Rednal or Rubery although in earlier years trams for Ladywood also boarded here. It is therefore interesting to find a view of a Permanent Way car running in the city centre. These single-deck trams were usually old tramcars, which when withdrawn, were fitted with two carborundum stones used to eradicate corrugations in the track by scrubbing the rail surface. Fixed to each side of the centre of the truck frame, these stones could be lowered on to the rails by means of rods and levers operated by a wheel. The PW cars had in their saloons four large water tanks to lubricate the operation.

PW9 was formerly ex-CBT 166 and was built as an open-top, open-vestibule, double-decker in 1903 by ER&TCW. It became 509 when acquired by the Corporation in July 1911, then in October 1916 was rebuilt as a single-deck non-powered trailer, initially behind car 431 on the Nechells route, then, from March 1917 until 1918, behind ex-CBT

bogie car 451 on the Washwood Heath route. It then lay unused until December 1928 when it became PW9.

This 1951 view shows it running in full fleet livery on the outer line in Navigation Street, which bypassed the loading loop at the shelters. Behind is the old Birmingham Technical School, opened in December 1895 and later the Central Grammar School. This terracotta-faced building was in nearby Suffolk Street, and dominated the skyline here throughout the tramway era until it became a victim of the Suffolk Street Queensway inner ring road scheme. A further sign of the post-war changes in the transport scene at this time is the distant bus, a 1950 Daimler CVD6 of the 2031-2130 Class working the replacement 48 route through Balsall Heath to the Maypole terminus beyond Kings Heath. *F. N. Lloyd Jones*

Above right Standing alongside the steel, wrought-iron and glass-roofed passenger shelters in Navigation Street is car 317. This UEC-bodied open-balconied tramcar entered service in spring 1911, and is working on the 70 service to Rednal. Rated at 40hp and mounted on UEC Preston 'flexible-axle, swing-yoke' 7ft 6in trucks, it would remain allocated to Selly Oak depot until May 1939, when it and other class-mates were replaced by bogie tramcars made redundant from Hockley depot by the closure of the West Bromwich, Wednesbury and Dudley routes. As the Rednal service to the Lickey Hills had only been introduced on 12 July 1927, it was still enjoying huge passenger numbers as Birmingham folk travelled to the local beauty spot. The crowds, often four rows deep on Bank Holidays and summer weekends, frequently needed the shade of the tram shelters, although, knowing the vagaries of the English climate, it was probably to escape the rain. *M. J. O'Connor*

Below The Bristol Road and Cotteridge trams turned sharp right into John Bright Street from Navigation Street, and car 622, a 1920 Brush-bodied 60-seater with Brush Burnley maximum traction bogies and DK30/1L 63hp motors, negotiates this curve in June 1952. This all-electric tram was one of ten to travel across the city from Miller Street depot during these last two months of tramcar operation at Selly Oak depot as at least seven of Selly Oak's trams had been taken out of service prematurely, leaving the depot decidedly short of stock. The body of 622 was considerably altered in its 33-year working life; originally built with open balconies, it was totally enclosed in July 1928 when it received the revised layout of eight windows per side in the upper saloon. In 1948 it was one of nine of the 587-636 Class to have its body strengthened, and this is evident in this view from the plated-over top-light windows at the extreme ends of the lower saloon. *R. Brook*

Below Turning from Navigation Street into John Bright Street is car 512, the first of the 75 bogie cars ordered in 1913, on the 35 short-working along Bristol Street to Selly Oak. It is about to cross the single-line junction that enabled Moseley Road cars, with their terminus in Hill Street and the railway station end of Navigation Street, to link with the trams coming from the Suffolk Street side of Navigation Street. This was also the track used by the Hagley Road and Ladywood trams as they started at the Queens Hotel end of Navigation Street, before crossing into John Bright Street and eventually reaching Hagley Road at Five Ways. Car 512 was one of the 70hp trams that had bodies rebuilt in about 1948; this could be easily identified as all the cars so treated had their platform bulkhead windows plated over.

This 1949 view was taken when the Hill Street bridge over the north-western end of New Street Station was being rebuilt. Daimler COG5 11187 (FOF 187) is glimpsed at the bottom of Hill Street and is crossing the temporary bridge above the railway lines. In those days

Hill Street was considered a fearsome climb with a fully laden bus, up under the bridge linking the two halves of the General Post Office and into Victoria Square. The clock tower just visible is known as 'Big Brum' and was designed by Yeoville Thomason in 1885 as part of the City Museum & Art Gallery building. Today the pedestrianised John Bright Street is a far cry from when it was one of the busiest city centre streets used by the trams. *F. N. Lloyd Jones*

Bottom Car 516 travels away from Navigation Street past the bomb-damaged corner of John Bright Street at the junction with Hill Street on its way to Rednal. John Bright Street was named after a Victorian Member of Parliament; constructed in 1881, it opened up access to the south-west of the city centre, replacing the Inkleys Greens Village and Cross Street, in which were some of the most violent and notorious slums in Birmingham. In the foreground is the pointwork that connected the eastern end of Navigation Street to John Bright Street, used latterly for Selly Oak cars to gain access to Kyotts Lake Road works. However, after the Moseley Road abandonments that depot's connection to the Bristol Road for the Lickey Hills extras was no longer required, and a new crossover direct from the western end of Navigation Street into Hill Street was constructed in April 1950.

This area of John Bright Street and Hill Street was very badly damaged on the night of 19/20 November 1940. A landmine destroyed the Malt Shovel public house on the island site between the two streets. By early 1950, when this view was taken, the site was still derelict, and it would be more than ten years before it was redeveloped. *D. Sanders collection*

Opposite top The early post-war Riley Pathfinder has swept past 63hp tram 741 in John Bright Street near the junction with Smallbrook Street. In the distance is Horse Fair, and beyond that the main A38 Bristol Road to Selly Oak and Northfield. The stylish Riley, virtually the only car in sight, epitomised the last mass-produced cars to have streamlined wings and running boards. Inbound trams went from Horse Fair into Suffolk Street, to the right of this view. Most of the buildings behind the tram were demolished as part of the Smallbrook Ringway scheme; begun in 1957, this was the first section of the Inner Ring Road to be completed, opened on 11 March 1960 by the Rt Hon Ernest Marples MP.

Car 741 entered service in November 1926 and belonged to the first class of cars, numbered 732-761, to be equipped with EMB Maley air-

track and magnetic brakes. Originally allocated to Rosebery Street depot for the 33 route to Ladywood and the 34 route along the Hagley Road, it was transferred to Selly Oak in June 1934 and remained there until it was withdrawn in May 1952. *R. T. Wilson*

Middle Further up Suffolk Street, car 522 climbs the rise from the end of Station Street in company with a 1949 Vauxhall Wyvern, and in front of a splendid 1936 Austin Eighteen. From this vantage point Suffolk Street looked fairly flat, yet the road dropped quite sharply before rising to the distant buildings of the civic centre. The tram is one of 75 cars built in 1913 with UEC bodies mounted on Mountain & Gibson Burnley maximum-traction bogies and equipped with DK19A 40hp Dick, Kerr motors. Originally fitted with open balconies, the class was totally enclosed between May 1926 and September 1931, and car 522 was one of ten to receive a new top-cover in about 1929, which provided eight windows per side instead of the original four, to the same design as the contemporary 762-811 Class. It was modified in 1927 with GEC WT32R 70hp motors, and in this form was ideally suited to the fast running along Bristol Road's reserved track. Seen here in around 1949, still with the pre-war style of fleet number, it is working the 71 route into the city from Rubery. It was not taken out of service until the final abandonment of the Bristol Road routes on 5 July 1952, along with all the other 70hp cars, being broken up at Witton depot the same month. *F. N. Lloyd Jones*

Bottom Struggling through the snow at the Horse Fair-Holloway Head junction in Suffolk Street heading for the city during the appalling weather of December 1940 is Brush-bodied Brush-Burnley maximum-traction-bogied tram 620, working on the 35 route from Selly Oak. Car 620 had only been a Selly Oak-allocated tram since June the previous year, having been at Hockley depot until the abandonment of the Handsworth group of routes in April 1939.

Behind the tram and towering above the single-storey premises of the Westminster Bank on the left is the elaborately styled Bulls Head public house on corner of Horse Fair and Smallbrook Street, designed by the late-Victorian Birmingham-based architects James & Lister Lea. Following the tram is a snow-covered Morris Twelve Series III dating from 1938 or 1939. *Birmingham Central Reference Library*

Above Although a major road, Smallbrook Street was only ever used for public transport by Midland Red buses. Car 808, one of the bow-collector cars recently transferred from Washwood Heath depot, leaves John Bright Street and, just beyond the bollard in the foreground, will meet the inbound line of the Bristol Road group of routes on their way to the Navigation Street terminus. In this 1951 view the tram is in the final post-war livery and carries on its side the Co-op's famous 'Say CWS and Save' advertisement. The tram was to see service until the closure of the Bristol Road routes on 5 July 1952, and was broken up at Witton depot later the same month. All the air-brake cars, despite having been built in 1926 and after, were broken up at this time as the drivers of the Aston Road group of routes worked the earlier, lower-horsepower all-electric-braked trams; it was considered inappropriate to retrain them on the newer air-brake cars for just one year's extra service. *C. Carter*

Below The tram stop at the junction of Smallbrook Street (to the right) and Holloway Head (beyond the tall building to the left) in Horse Fair was located in the middle of this important thoroughfare. Car 543 is inbound on the 71 route from Rubery and will turn left after passing outward-bound car 560, on the 35 route short-working to Selly Oak. In this bustling 1949 scene, the tramcar still appears to be the main mode of public transport, at least in this part of Birmingham. It seems as permanent as the sign for the products of the Rootes Group; the names Humber, Hillman, Sunbeam-Talbot, Commer and Karrier were to disappear in the 1960s and 1970s together with the building carrying the hoarding.

The rather down-at-heel Ford Ten Tudor on the left (signifying 'Two Door' rather than any connection with Henry VIII!) looks as though it won't last much longer. It is passing the City of Birmingham Salvage Department's Morrison Electricars VC40C two-ton dustcart 210 (EVP 810), built in 1939. Perhaps surprisingly, it was the dustcart that would be the longest survivor in the photograph, lasting until withdrawal in the mid-1960s. *F. N. Lloyd Jones*

Opposite top Brick Kiln Lane had been associated with a horse fair and a general market since 1777, then was developed in 1792 and renamed Horse Fair in 1812; its wide street was used as a horse market until the early years of the 20th century. Passing Lion House, occupied by drysalter George Hull on the corner of Horse Fair and Essex Street, car 733, one of Selly Oak depot's EMB air-brake trams of 1926 vintage, is working out of the city to Rednal on the 70 route, while car 822 is travelling into the city from Cotteridge. Following 733 and passing the shoe shop of A & M Forstag is a pre-war two-door Vauxhall saloon, which seems to carry a Birmingham re-registration dating from July 1951. *W. A. Camwell*

Middle In August 1951 car 802 has just turned from Horse Fair into Bristol Street on its way to Rednal on the 70 route. In the far distance is a 1949 Daimler CVD6 with a Metro-Cammell body, working on a Special duty; these buses were some of the quietest and most refined of all Birmingham's post-war bus fleet and were popular with drivers and passengers alike. All the buildings on the right were demolished in the 1960s when Bristol Street and Horse Fair were widened to become dual carriageways. This included St Catherine of Sienna, a Victorian Gothic Roman Catholic church, built in the mid-19th century, but extended with an enlarged chancel in 1890. All the shops to the left of the tram still remain, although now they are mainly occupied by high-quality Indian restaurants. *R. T. Wilson*

Bottom The Birmingham-registered 1936 Morris Twelve-Four is held up by trams 792 and 534, which are both leaving the city fully laden in Bristol Street, at its junction with Bromsgrove Street. In the distance an unidentified 762 Class car works inbound on the 70 route. With the exception of St Luke's church in the background, virtually all the buildings in this view remain today, including the splendid row of art nouveau shops just beyond car 534. The selection of trams in this view represents the three main types used on the Bristol Road services during the last two years of operation. All have either 63hp or 70hp motors capable of maintaining well over 35mph on the reserved track, while

car 792 and the other eight-windowed tram are both equipped with EMB air-brakes. If there was a criticism of tramcar development by the Tramways Department it was that it stagnated once the basic design had been produced in 1913, with the 512 Class of bogie trams. Car 534 belongs to this earlier design, but in the course of rebuilding it became virtually indistinguishable from the later tramcars, such as the eight-windowed 792, which was built with only minor modifications some 15 years later. *R. T. Wilson*

Below The CBT converted the battery accumulator operation to Bournbrook to overhead current collection from 14 May 1901. The tram leaving the city centre along Bristol Street is CBT car 162, one of the original ER&TCW open-top, reverse-staircase trams built in 1901 with Peckham cantilever 6-foot-wheelbase trucks. In 1911 this tram was taken over by the Corporation, becoming car 507 and being refitted with Brill 21E trucks during the first six months of 1913. The ornate traction poles in Bristol Street were placed in the centre of the road, unique in Birmingham and almost as though intended to placate the Gough-Calthorpe family, who were against the intrusion of electric overhead wires despoiling their elegant Calthorpe estate; however, normal span wires were installed after about eight years of Company operation.

A man carries a large hunk of meat, while a liberated Edwardian lady cycles out of the picture on the right. Nearly all the shops on the right have their canvas sun-blinds pulled down; is the man standing on top of the little gantry beside the tram painting his shop front? On the other side of the wide expanse of Bristol Street is the ornate tower of the aforementioned St Catherine of Sienna Roman Catholic Church, built in 1875 to the designs of architects Dunn & Hansom and demolished for road-widening in 1964 with all the buildings on the left, being replaced by an ultra-modern circular brick and concrete church in 1965. *Author's collection*

Bottom After the takeover of the Bristol Road routes from the CBT on 1 July 1911, the Corporation's newest trams were used. As the former CBT depot at Bournbrook still contained the numerous sub-standard open-top cars and there was not enough room for any of the new stock, the routes along Bristol Road were at first operated partly from Moseley Road depot. On a hot summer's day in 1911, not long after the BCT takeover, a lady with a parasol starts to cross Bristol Street near the junction with Belgrave Road. The distant tram is one of the newly introduced UEC-built 301 Class cars, still in original condition with the large offside vestibule window. The characteristic metal cowl, a well-known Birmingham feature necessary to give sufficient clearance over the brake handle, has not yet been fitted; for their first eight or so months in service the 301-360 batch of cars retained their original vertical handbrake handles, and it was only on being converted to horizontal handbrake wheels that the cars were altered. It will be seen when comparing this view with that of 552 opposite, separated by the Great War, that the original CBT bracket arms were shorter, which necessitated the trams' trolleypoles being extended

ver the kerb far more. *Commercial postcard*

Top On a typical Edwardian day, when the sun always seemed to be shining, CBT car 167, well loaded with passengers, is coming into the city with the Trees Inn just visible through the foliage on the right. The tram is standing in Bristol Road with Spring Vale on the right; on the extreme left, where the two young lads and the little girl are standing, is the start of Belgrave Road, which led to the nearby Balsall Heath group of tram routes, opened in 1907. Car 167, built at the end of 1901, was not one of the 17 taken over by the Corporation on 1 July 1911, as it was transferred to the Yardley and Aston remnants of the CBT system until the end of that year. At this point it was transferred to the Birmingham & Midland Tramways Joint Committee – but that was in the future! *Author's collection*

Middle Cloche-hatted women and straw-boatered and cloth-capped men go about their business in Bristol Street in the early 1920s, when this main road out of the city was a bustling commercial suburban shopping area. Although only about half a mile from the city centre, it has the tree-lined prosperity generally lacking at that time on the other main roads into the city. Brush-built tram 552, working the 36 route to Cotteridge and still in its original condition with open balconies, passes the junction with St Lukes Road beneath the delicate tracery of the overhead bracket supports. Although the Bristol Street route had the advantages of being double-track, the overhead was still suspended from the rather ornate side-bracket arms. By the middle of the 1920s this had generally been replaced by span wires. *Commercial postcard*

Bottom Car 342 is seen here on 26 November 1938 at the compulsory stop at Belgrave Road when working the 72 route, a short-working that went as far as Longbridge and the Austin Motor Works. 'The Armoured Car', as it was nicknamed, had been running since January 1921 with the prototype experimental design of covered vestibule; this had been fitted as a temporary measure, as totally enclosed, four-wheeled, double-deck tramcars were officially not allowed on narrow-gauge systems by the Board of Trade, because it

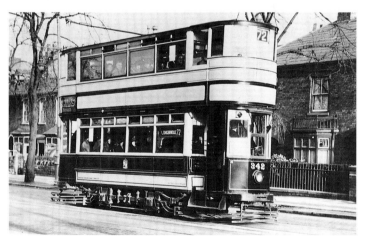

increased their instability. Car 342, with its rather awkwardly styled balcony windows, remained in service until 30 September 1950, but is seen here in the splendid post-1931 livery, fully lined out in blue and gold, although the earlier version also had the window pillars lined out. *L. W. Perkins*

Top Only one of the Washwood Heath bow-collector cars, 785, failed to live out a full working life. In April 1941 a bomb badly damaged cars 781, 785, 786 and 809 at the depot, having fallen between 785 and 786; the latte was kept throughout the remainder of the war befor being repaired using parts from 785's good end. It re

entering service in February 194 and, now fitted with a trolley pol after being transferred to Selly Oa depot in October 1950, crests the ris of Bristol Road at Wellington Road just beyond the ABC Bristol Roa cinema at the Spring Vale-Belgrav Road junction. It is working the 7 route to Rubery, and this sectio went through land owned by th Calthorpe family; according to th novelist Francis Brett Young, th Calthorpe estate was 'an area of tree lined roads and exquisitely tastefu houses, tennis courts and croque lawns, rose trees and rhododendro bushes...' The mid-19th-centur houses to the right of the tram on th Balsall Heath side of the road wer built to provide an area of good quality housing along Bristol Roa but by the early 1950s they wer falling into a fairly sorry state an would only survive until the end c the decade, being replaced by moder maisonettes and flats in the earl 1960s. By way of contrast, on th extreme left is Wellington Road, on of the most prestigious addresses i Edgbaston where the Regency an early Victorian houses stood in thei own grounds, reflecting an opulenc that has been sustained only in thi part of the Calthorpe estate. *R. Wilson*

Middle and bottom The origina trams that opened the overhea electric tram service along Bristo Road were those owned by CBT. Ca 163 was built in 1901 by ER&TCV and was an open-topped, reverse staircase double-decker, seating 4 passengers and mounted on Peckha 9A cantilever trucks. Numbered 15 165, the class had two BTH GE 5 6T 37hp motors. Car 163 is seen i Bristol Road, Edgbaston, in 190 passing through the high prosperous suburban arcadia of th Calthorpe estate. The tram is on it way to Bournbrook, where th original accumulator tram terminated; CBT extended the rout to the new terminus at Chapel Lan Selly Oak, on 14 May 1901. Car 16 was not taken over by BCT in Ju 1911, being transferred to Compan premises on about New Year's Da 1912, after which its subsequen career is not precisely recorded.

A century or so later, on 7 October 2002, travelling into the city centre, is a brand new Travel West Midlands double-decker, albeit out of service. No 4355 (BX 02 AVL), a Dennis 'Trident' SFD334 with an Alexander 147/28F body, entered service in July 2002 and is about to pass the junction with Sir Harry's Road. It is adorned with the 'Jubilee Line' livery, commemorating the 50th anniversary of the abandonment of the Bristol Road and Cotteridge tram routes on 5 July 1952. This section of Bristol Road has largely retained its character, particularly with the unchanged houses off the picture to the right, which are on the land still owned by the paternally protective Calthorpe estate. The housing on the other side of the tree-lined Bristol Road have not been so lucky, with a pleasant, if somewhat unplanned, series of 1970s housing developments. *Commercial postcard, via A. D. Packer/D. R. Harvey*

Top The advantage of the tramcar in adverse weather conditions could not be better shown than in this wartime scene in Edgbaston. In the atrocious snowstorms of January 1940, the city's tramcars not only kept going, but also cleared the snow for the benefit of other traffic. Car 635, a Brush-bodied 62-seater with 63hp motors, entered service in March 1921, and had only been at Selly Oak depot for just over one month when the snows arrived. Here it is ploughing its way out of the city through the slush in Bristol Road approaching the Pebble Mill Road junction where the Pershore Road trams, working on the 36 service to Cotteridge, turned left. It is working on the 70 route to Rednal and is about to enter the first section of reserved track along Bristol Road. Car 635 was rarely photographed and its early withdrawal for scrapping on 3 October 1950 did not help its slightly elusive career. The only other vehicle on the road is an Austin K2 lorry with only its off-side headlight masked. *Birmingham Central Reference Library*

Above CBT replaced its accumulator battery bogie trams and opened the overhead electric tram service between Suffolk Street and the extension from Dawlish Road, Bournbrook, to Chapel Lane, Selly Oak, on 14 May 1901. Within three years the original ER&CTW cars were proving to be too small for the successful new service and were in part replaced by some of CBT's latest trams. Car 209 was the first of eight double-deck, open-top cars built by CBT at Kyotts Lake Road Works in Sparkbrook in late 1904, all equipped with unsuccessful Lycett & Conaty 8ft 6in radial trucks; they were also somewhat underpowered, with two 25hp Brush 1002D motors. It was allocated to Bournbrook depot and stayed there throughout the tramway upheavals of 1907-11, then was transferred to the Birmingham & Midland Joint Committee on 3 August 1911 for further use in the Black Country. It is standing in Bristol Road some time after the route to Cotteridge had been opened on 20 May 1904 as far as Breedon Cross; these are the tracks curving to the left over which the intrepid lady cyclist is pedalling. On the right, next to the post-box, are the lodge gates to the long tree-lined drive up to Park Grove House. This impressive Georgian house was one of a number of 18th-century houses located around the grounds of Edgbaston Hall; dating from 1717, it survives today as the headquarters of Edgbaston Golf Club. *Commercial postcard*

Top Beyond Priory Road was the first section of reserved track in Bristol Road, and within 200 yards was the junction where the Cotteridge cars, working the 36 route, turned left into Pebble Mill Road. Car 742, one of the 1926 Brush-built EMB air-brake bogie cars, is on the inbound line just on the city side of this junction at the Bundy clocks that stood between the tram tracks in the middle of the central reservation. These were used by the platform staff to 'clock in' they also recorded the time-keeping of the services, and were only phased out by West Midlands Passenger Transport in the 1980s. The uniformed schoolchildren seem to be playing around, but on today's A38 road such frolics would be virtually impossible, if not suicidal, as this is one of the busiest of Birmingham's main arterial roads. The Midland Red bus is a BMMO S8 with an MCCW body and is working the 14.. route to Bromsgrove via West Heath and Barnt Green. *R. T. Wilson*

Middle Car 630 speeds across the Pebble Mill Road junction on the 72 route on 25 June 1952. The conductor, with Bell Punch ticket machine and leather money bag strapped over his summer dust jacket, looks out of the entrance towards the approaching tram stop at the city end of the dual carriageway run from Selly Oak. The tram is one of the 587-636 Class built in 1920 by Brush with a four window, vestibuled-platform body with open balconies, Brush Burnley maximum-traction bogies and GE 249A 37hp motors. Birmingham's Tramway Department became interested in improving the braking performance of the tram fleet, and as a result car 630 was fitted with EMB Maley air-brakes in June 1923, and later with the more powerful DK30/1L 63hp motors. It was used as the prototype for the later air brake bogie cars more usually associated with the Ladywood and Bristol Road routes; these were the 732-761 Class, built in 1926 and fitted from new with air-brakes. Latterly, 630 ran alongside the newer air-brake cars, being variously allocated to Rosebery Street, Washwood Heath and finally Selly Oak depots. It was always the odd one out among the air-brake bogi tram fleet, but unlike some 19 of the same 587 Class that survived until the final abandonment of the Birmingham system on 4 July 1953, car 630 was broken up with all the other surviving air-brake cars in July 1952 after the Bristol Road abandonment. *L. W. Perkins*

Opposite bottom The pre-war livery, with its cream rocker panels and large shaded numerals, was replaced in 1946, and all the remaining enclosed bogie cars were repainted in the simplified post-war style. A fairly late survivor in the dignified earlier livery was car 744, photographed in August 1948 about to cross the gap in the central reservation where the Cotteridge-bound trams turned into Pebble Mill Road, off the photograph to the right. Car 744 was one of few of the 1926 Brush-bodied, EMB air-brake cars to be allocated to three depots: originally allocated to Rosebery Street for use on the Hagley Road and Ladywood services, in the 1930s it was also used at Selly Oak and Washwood Heath before finally settling at Selly Oak in January 1940. Unfortunately, it was involved in a severe accident in July 1942 and was stored in Sampson Road paint shop from November 1943 until June 1945. It had the distinction of being the only Birmingham tram stored there to escape the breakers' torch and be returned to service, still in the pre-war livery. *D. Griffiths*

Top right The tree-lined central reservation along sections of the Bristol Road enabled the bogie trams equipped with higher-horsepower motors to achieve speeds of well over 40mph. Car 587 was another of the

587-636 Class built by Brush in 1920 (see opposite), and this photograph was taken about 30 years later, by which time the car's original motors had been replaced by Dick, Kerr DK 30/1 63hp ones and its balconies had been enclosed. This was the tram that overturned in Suffolk Street in 1942 (see page 17), and no doubt as a result became one of nine of the class requiring to have its body strengthened. It was one of only 19 tramcars to be transferred in July 1952 for further service on the final Erdington group of routes, and was finally withdrawn on the last day of tramway operation in the city, 4 July 1953. *C. Carter*

Above right While central reservation running in Leeds, Glasgow and Liverpool was feted as the best in the UK, the reserved track along Bristol Road is frequently forgotten but should be placed in the same category! The reserved sections were constructed between 1923 and 1927, remembered today in the breeze rustling through the now mature trees. Speeds of 40mph were regularly reached on the dual-carriageway sections of the 8.19 route miles to Rednal on the 70 route; remember that this was on the much narrower 3ft 6in gauge. Car 734, the third of the 30-strong Brush-bodied, 63hp EMB air-braked bogie cars built in 1926 and originally allocated to Rosebery Street depot for the Ladywood 33 route, speeds along the reserved track towards the city centre in the winter of 1951. It has just entered the section of reserved track at Edgbaston Park Road and is passing a 'School' road sign, for beyond the tram and to the left of the parked car are the grounds of King Edward's School. Car 734 is heading towards Eastern Road, where it would be parked on the Saturday of the abandonment, 5 July 1952, and not driven away to Witton depot for scrapping until the 18th, when it was one of 20 to travel under its own power to meet its fate at the hands of the acetylene burners of W. T. Bird. *R. T. Wilson*

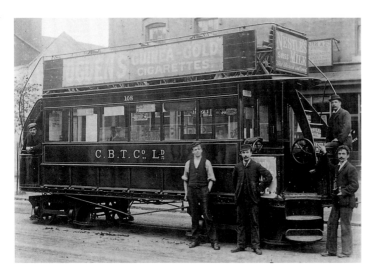

Above Cars 781 and 737 stand forlornly on the Bristol Road reserved carriageway at Eastern Road on 8 July 1952, the Tuesday after the abandonment of the route. It had been decided to break up all the air-brake cars at Witton depot, but because it had a capacity of only about 40 trams, 54 cars, formerly allocated to Selly Oak and Cotteridge depots, were stored on this central reservation between Pebble Mill Road and Eastern Road, gradually being transferred to Witton depot as the breaking up got under way. The very last car to be removed, 513, left on 23 July. There was a watchman on duty to guard the trams, but it is quite remarkable that virtually no vandalism took place in the middle of one of Birmingham's principal roads! However, the destination box and headlight of car 781 did disappear to a souvenir-hunter on the evening of the final closure. *T. J. Edgington*

Middle Loading up with passengers in the middle of Bristol Road, Bournbrook, today would be considered suicidal, but in 1952 traffic levels were much lower and cars just patiently waited for the tram to pick up its passengers. Car 762, the first of the former Washwood Heath bow-collector tramcars, built by Brush on EMB Burnley maximum-traction bogies and fitted with air-brakes and 63hp motors, is working towards Selly Oak on the 71 service to Rubery. To the right is Dawlish Road, where the depot buil n 1890 for the CBT accumulator ars was located. Converted to lectric tram operation in 1901, it emained operational until Selly Oak lepot was opened on 11 July 1927.

Although today the nearby Jniversity of Birmingham has an normous influence over ournbrook's accommodation and ocial life, in 1952 it was a different ituation. On the right is Clarence lackwell's greengrocery business, lthough he also sold chicken and hat cheap delicacy of the early post-var years, rabbit. The tall 18th-entury building alongside the tram is he old Bournbrook Tavern. The notorcycle, probably an Ariel, arked on the left, was first registered round January 1952, suggesting hat this photograph was taken in the arly months of that year. Ariels were nanufactured in Grange Road, vhich was to the left of the Belisha eacon that stood outside the old ournbrook Hotel. *W. A. Camwell*

Opposite bottom The first electric ram route along Bristol Road was opened by the BCT on 24 July 1890, nd was operated by the largest fleet f battery accumulator trams in the ountry, some 14 being used on the ervice between Suffolk Street and the ournbrook terminus at Dawlish Road. Cars 101-112 were eight-wheel open-top bogie trams built by the alcon Engine & Car Works of oughborough and were very similar

n design to the cable-cars that operated on the Snow Hill o Handsworth line. They seated 48 passengers and were perated from a depot in Dawlish Road, which was ventually taken over in 1911 by the Corporation. Despite he problems of battery operation, which included sluggish erformance and leaking acid, the trams worked until eplacement by conventional overhead electric cars on 14 May 1901. The pioneering nature of this experimental ervice, although not without its critics at the time, must ave been reasonably successful, as it lasted for nearly 11 ears! Car 108 is seen in Bristol Road, Bournbrook, in CBT ownership in about 1897. The six hinged doors ontaining the batteries form the tram's rocker panel. *Dr I. W. Whitcombe collection, Science Museum, London*

Top right The trams' lead-acid batteries were withdrawn rom behind the rocker panels on trays and exchanged very day with recharged batteries; the clever replacement ystem from being on charge to being in the cradle on the ramcar only took around half an hour. An ingenious utomatic electrical connection was made in the tram by he use of sprung brass clips connected to the car wiring. ach tram had a series of batteries consisting of 96 cells, vhich gave a current of around 192 volts. The recharging rocess, which charged the batteries up to their maximum

capacity of 350 amps, took about 10 hours. The Dawlish Road depot had these two charging gantries, onto which the trams were driven; their foundations went down about 15 feet in order to support the recharging trams. The trams ran a 15-minute service, except for five days: on 30 January 1895 there was a severe fire on the accumulator room, and the service was suspended until 4 February. Horse-buses were substituted until repairs were completed and an initial 20-minute service could be resumed. Cars 104 and 103 are in the Charging Station in Dawlish Road depot in 1891. *ECC*

Above On a miserable Wednesday 12 April 1939, car 752 is about to leave the Dawlish Road compulsory stop in Bristol Road on the climb up to Selly Oak, outside the Ten Acres & Stirchley Co-operative Society's (TASCO) grocery and provisions store. TASCO was a separate Co-operative Society in Birmingham and ran a chain of shops in the south-west of the city that remained independent of the nearby much larger Birmingham Co-operative Society until the early 1970s. Car 752 belonged to the first class of 30 trams in Birmingham to be fitted with air-brakes, and was to serve the Bristol Road routes for about 19 years. It is in the standard, rather dignified pre-war lined-out livery and is working the 71 route to Rubery. *H. B. Priestley*

Selly Oak

Below Located just on the city side of the former Midland Railway's bridge at Selly Oak between Heeley Road, alongside the entrance to Selly Oak railway station, and Hubert Road (hidden by the tramcar) was the Selly Oak Institute. This mock-half-timbered building was opened in 1894 at a cost of £5,500, donated by George Cadbury, the well-known chocolate manufacturer and philanthropist; it was in the same style as the buildings being constructed at the same time in his own Bournville Village. The tram is car 167, numerically the second of six open-top, 48-seater double-deckers built by CBT itself at Kyotts Lake Road in late 1901 to supplement the original 151-165 trams, and virtually identical to these first ER&TCW tramcars. It is climbing the hill towards the terminus at the junction with Chapel Lane about a quarter of a mile away. *Author's collection*

Bottom On Thursday 5 May 1949 car 743 is passed by a Bedford van on the inside as it rushes towards Selly Oak. Bristol Road in Bournbrook was also known as High Street, and in the days of CBT and its battery accumulator trams, the terminus was at the bottom of the hill at Dawlish Road. Car 743 has stopped on this hill between the original terminus and the Selly Oak terminus at Chapel Lane, to which it was extended on 14 May 1901. It is parked outside a teashop next to the Institute where the crew usually got their white enamel billy-can filled with tea. The driver might drink a cupful while driving; the rest would be consumed once the terminus was reached. Just behind the tram is the 'Friends' Institute' again. *J. E. Cull*

Opposite above A little beyond the Institute was the railway bridge that took the former Midland Railway Birmingham and West Suburban railway line over the Bristol Road. It had a restricted height and the trams suitable for this route carried a cast metal plaque that read 'This car can run on Aston & Rednal routes' or 'Low Bridge Car. Selly Oak, Aston, Dudley Port' as appropriate. Car 534, one of the GEC WT32R 70hp remotored trams, had been repainted in June 1949 and its well-varnished paintwork shines in the sunlight. In view of the fact that the tram had only two more years of service in front of it, it is surprising that it had its body strengthened after this, when overhauled on 23 June 1950. The tram is working the 71 route to Rubery and is about to go beneath the bridge on its way from the city, having just passed the stationary Morris Commercial PV-type van. A Guy Vixen lorry is emerging from the shadows of the bridge. *Lens of Sutton*

16040 SELLY OAK INSTITUTE.

Below Emerging from the bridge, Brush-built EMB air-brake car 748 powers up the hill from Bournbrook while working the 71 route on 17 June 1952, towards the end of its 26-year service life. Note that its trolley-pole is extended to the kerb-side in order to be low enough to clear the bridge. Dares Ales were produced at Dares's South End brewery in Belgrave Road, which was taken over by the nearby Davenports in 1961; ironically its site, now in Belgrave Middleway, is today occupied by the Birmingham Central Mosque! Beyond the bridge can be seen the imposing edifice of Birmingham University, opened on 7 July 1909 by King Edward VII and Queen Alexandra. Its almost Byzantine basilica-styled domed Great Hall, coupled with the just visible slender campanile, modelled on the 14th-century Torre del Mangia at Sienna, stand on a hill in Edgbaston. The distant academic heights are a world apart from the busy street scene with the advertisement for Joe Loss at the Birmingham Hippodrome offering a less cerebral type of entertainment. *R. Brook*

Top The original suburban terminus of the new CBT overhead electric tram service was at the Plough & Harrow public house in Selly Oak. This extension from the accumulator tram terminus at Dawlish Road, Bournbrook, took the trams into Selly Oak for the first time. Standing here in about 1908, having driven into the stub track opposite the junction with Chapel Lane, is CBT car 163, one of the original 15 trams, numbered 151-165, built by ER&TCW and delivered to the company in the spring of 1901. The driver and conductor pose at the front of the tram before heading back to Birmingham and the loop around Suffolk Street, which had been introduced in 1902. Car 163 was not taken over by the Corporation but was transferred to the Birmingham & Midland Joint Committee on 1 or 2 January 1912. *Commercial postcard*

Middle Cars 524 and 737, running into Selly Oak depot after the rush hour on an autumn day in 1951, have arrived from the outer terminus and reversed in order to turn into Chapel Lane. This junction was dominated by three buildings, all of which offered in a variety of ways welcoming hospitality or entertainment. Opposite the road junction stood St John's Methodist Church, built in 1876 and closed for worship in about 1959. Next to the tram is the curved face of the Plough & Harrow public house, opened in 1900 as the New Inn. Behind the photographer is the 1,200-seat Oak Cinema, opened in 1924 with a showing of *Chu Chin Chow*; only a few months before this photograph was taken it had been voted the second cleanest cinema in the country. Alas, nearly all has gone today in a road-widening scheme that has largely removed the Selly Oak bottleneck on the Outer Ring Road and transferred it just down the hill towards the city in Bournbrook. The chapel was demolished in the late 1970s after being used for a number of non-secular functions; the Plough & Harrow went the same way in the early 1980s and the Oak was pulled down in December 1984. *R. T. Wilson*

Bottom A slightly unkempt car 784 turns into Bristol Road from Chapel

Lane on the last morning of services to Rednal and Rubery. The few people walking about that day scarcely give the trams a second glance, but by the following morning their service would be operated by buses. It would not be quite the end for the former Washwood Heath bow-collector, Brush-built air-brake car of 1928, however; it would be stored on the Bristol Road central reservation from the cessation of the evening service until the final movements of trams from there on Thursday 23 July, when, together with 19 other trams, it was driven to Kyotts Lake Road for scrapping (see page 30). *A. K. Terry*

Above right In this further view of the Plough & Harrow corner, Harborne garage's AEC Matador 0853 No 14 is involved in the recovery of the damaged vehicles following an accident between tramcar 595, a Brush-built car of 1920, and an ex-Army Austin K6 4x4 on 5 June 1950. The accident blocked the Selly Oak junction for several hours. The ex-RAF Matador was acquired in January 1948, and although in this case it was carrying the trade plate 1620 O, it usually had the trade plate number 924 OP. After withdrawal it was acquired for preservation. *J. E. Cull*

Below Chapel Lane was only used for depot workings by the trams allocated to Selly Oak depot, and on 7 June 1952 cars 767 and 518 have climbed the hill to join Bristol Road at the Selly Oak junction. To the left of the trams is the Oak Cinema, while behind tram 767, which is about to turn towards the city centre, is the Plough & Harrow. Car 767 was one of the Brush-built, totally enclosed, EMB air-brake cars of 1928; it was mounted on EMB Burnley maximum-traction bogies and fitted with air-wheel, air-track and magnetic brake gear. Originally allocated to Washwood Heath depot, these trams' Dick, Kerr DK30/1L 63hp motors and Fischer bow collectors allowed them to give some very spirited performances along Washwood Heath Road; yet when transferred to Selly Oak they were not as popular with the staff because of their complicated braking system. Waiting at the bus stop in Chapel Lane while working on the 20 route to the City via the nearby Weoley Castle housing estate is 1545 (GOE 545), a Daimler CVA6 with an MCCW body, which entered service on 2 October 1947 and was to remain active until the last day of May 1962. *J. H. Meredith*

Above With its splendid Dutch-style gables and large entrance doors, Selly Oak depot had a capacity for about 80 trams on its ten roads. It was opened on 12 July 1927 and its capacity was a substantial improvement on the former CBT depot in Dawlish Road, opened in May 1901, which could only accommodate 46 trams. The extensions along Bristol Road from Selly Oak to Northfield on 1 October 1923, to Longbridge on 17 December of that year, to Rednal on 14 April 1924, and finally to Rubery on Monday 8 February 1926, meant that a larger fleet of trams was required, so a bigger depot was needed. It was built at the bottom of Chapel Lane in Harborne Lane and remained in operation as a tram depot until 5 July 1952, although it had also been a bus garage

since 2 January 1935. On 24 February 1952 cars 519 and 743 stand on the forecourt with 1657 (HOV 657), the second of the 100 Leyland Titan PD2/1s of 1948-49, which, like the two trams, was bodied by Brush. The three single-deckers are Leyland Tiger PS2/1s with Weymann B34F bodies, delivered in 1950 to replace the pre-war fleet of Daimler COG5 single-deckers. The only one that is identifiable, 2233 (JOJ 233), was to become the first member of the class to be withdrawn in 1962 after being hit by a fire engine in Northfield on 9 September 1961. Just visible inside the depot is car 757. With its windows painted out, this tram was used as a cleaners' room until 14 May 1952 while the depot was being converted into a bus garage. *T. J. Edgington*

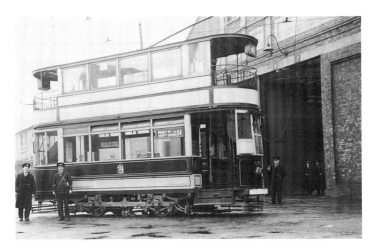

Left Former CBT car 240 was built at Kyotts Lake Road to a Brush design. New in 1904, it belonged to the class of trams known as the 'Aston' type; indeed, many of this type worked nearly all their Company careers on the Aston routes. Car 240, however, is known to have been at Bournbrook depot for a short time when nearly new, but by 1907 until the takeover of CBT by Birmingham Corporation on 1 January 1912, it was allocated, along with the other members of the class, to Witton. Some time after it had been taken into the BCT fleet it was renumbered 470. Originally it was an open-top car seating 26 on the outside and 22 in the lower saloon, and was fitted with Brush AA 6ft 6in-wheelbase trucks and two 25hp motors, but was totally rebuilt in 1925 to a vestibuled top-covered 35hp tram. It stands at the entrance to road 7 at Selly Oak depot early in 1938, in its final form shortly before withdrawal from service. *W. A. Camwell*

Right The village of Selly Oak was developed in the middle of the 19th century as a mixed industrial and residential area. The character of the suburb in the 1920s cannot have altered significantly since a large number of the Victorian buildings were still in residential use and not converted to shops. Car 375, working on the 35 route, stands at the terminus on the south side of Chapel Lane, which had replaced the original 1901 CBT terminus in 1923. In that year the route was extended along reserved track to the next important centre, the former village of Northfield. The tram has stopped opposite the Bundy clock and the driver, leaning against the tramcar, is waiting for the clock to come round to his departure time. In the foreground is the depot curve into Chapel Lane, which shows that the photograph was taken after July 1927 when Selly Oak depot was opened. Car 375 is one of the UEC 40hp four-wheelers of 1911, inherited by Selly Oak from Bournbrook in 1927, and remaining there with only one small break until August 1938. After being allocated mainly to Coventry Road and Miller Street depots for the next 12 years, it was withdrawn in September 1950. It had the distinction of being the last standard four-wheel tram, other than the preserved car 395, to be moved across Birmingham when it was transferred from Kyotts Lake Road Works to Witton depot for scrapping in November 1950. *Commercial postcard*

Below With the dreaded notice of impending abandonment in the balcony window, car 526, one of the last 19 of Selly Oak's rebuilt 70hp UEC cars of 1913, travels through Selly Oak working the 71 service to Rednal in late June 1952. It was one of 25 trams fitted with two GEC 32R motors in the first half of 1927, but due to the stress placed on the body by high-speed running along the reserved track of Bristol Road, it was rebuilt during 1948. This involved replacing the platform bulkhead windows with quarter-inch steel plating and flitch plates extending into the upper part of the lower saloon, thus eliminating the first lower saloon ventilator on each side. The tram has just left the compulsory stop halfway between Chapel Lane and Oak Tree Lane. In the background, behind the first Brush-built car 587 of 1920, is St John's Methodist Church on the corner of Elliott Road, while the white, flat-fronted building on the extreme left is the Dog & Partridge public house from around 1830. The tram is about to overtake a London-registered Austin Cambridge dating from November 1938. Behind the pollarded tree is a strange juxtaposition of shops: those owned by William Burton and G. A. Truman are both butchers! On the extreme right a little girl in a sun-hat appears to be walking through the ironmongery wares displayed on the pavement, probably to the displeasure of Arthur Green who owned the shop. *A. W. V. Mace/Mile Post 92½*

Selly Oak to Northfield and Longbridge

Below An almost full car 798 coasts into the top southern end of Selly Oak at the Oak Tree Lane junction on its way into the city from Rednal. It is was one of the 762-811 Class built by Brush in 1928 and mounted on EMB Burnley maximum-traction bogies. The arrangement of the wheels can be clearly seen in this view, taken on 10 July 1951: the larger 31½-inch driving wheels are at the outer end of the bogie, supporting the tram underframe, so about 85 per cent of the car's weight of 16¾ tons was available for accelerating and braking. With a capacity of 60 passengers, the stability of these large, thin-looking trams was dependent upon the performance of the bogies when travelling at up to 40mph on the narrow 3ft 6in-gauge reserved track. *J. E. Cull*

Bottom The climb out of Selly Oak continued for a few hundred yards but soon reached the first stretch of reserved track that extended to the crest of Griffins Hill at Weoley Park Road. Car 775, another of the ex-Washwood Heath bow-collector cars transferred to Bristol Road workings in October 1950, leaves Selly Oak working the 70 route from Rednal. The nature of the surrounding area changed quite suddenly from the distant structural heights of the 19th-century buildings to the mock-Elizabethan gabled semi-detached housing of the late 1920s. This was virtually the end of the housing development along Bristol Road until the edge of the suburb of Northfield was reached, just over 2 miles away. The intervening land was either owned by the Methodist Church's Selly Oak Colleges or by the Cadbury-owned Bournville Village Trust, and had generally been kept free of housing development. *R. F. Mack*

Opposite top Coming into Selly Oak on the 71 service from the distant Weoley Park Road on Tuesday 28 July 1931, open-balcony UEC tramcar 391 is travelling along the last section of reserved track in Bristol Road before it ended near Lodge Hill Road. Equipped with 7ft 6in 'flexible-yoke' trucks and two Dick, Kerr 40hp motors, the tram entered service early in 1912 and, for

a four-wheeler running on narrow-gauge track, was about as up-to-date as one could get. Twenty ears later, it still looks quite new in comparison with the contemporary cars of the early 1930s. This section of the dual carriageway opened on 1 October 1923 when the tram service to Northfield was opened as the 69 route. One question, though – what was a stagecoach doing travelling to Northfield in 1931...? *Birmingham Central Reference Library*

Middle On Tuesday 19 July 1938 Brush-bodied air-brake car 757 has just powered its way up Griffins Hill, Bristol Road South, from the distant valley of Griffins Brook at the bottom of the hill and is approaching Weoley Park Road. With two 63hp motors, the high-horsepower trams used on the reserved tracks of Bristol Road were capable of speeds in excess of 40mph, which meant that the petrol-engined Leyland 'Cub' half-cab coach labouring up the hill was being left far behind. To the left is the former home of George Cadbury Jnr, a large half-timber and brick house built in 1902, which in 1957 became Fircroft College, part of the Selly Oak teacher training colleges. Next door is the Woodbrooke Settlement for Religious and Social Study, which was funded by the Cadbury family and the Society of Friends. This 18th-century house had been the home of some of Birmingham's most distinguished industrial families including Josiah Mason, the Elkington family and George Cadbury Snr before conversion to a theological college. *W. A. Camwell*

Bottom One of Cotteridge's Short Brothers-built trams, 833, was used by Selly Oak depot for its final six weeks of service, and is seen here having just left the tram stop on Bristol Road's reserved track at Witherford Way. It is working the 70 route on its way into the city and is just beginning the climb up Griffins Hill opposite the abovementioned Fircroft. It is Saturday 5 July 1952 and the notices announcing the closure of the Bristol Road group of tram services are in the front balcony window. The somewhat reduced

standards of track maintenance are visible as 833 kicks up dust as it accelerates towards the city. Beyond, at the top of the hill, the laying of pipes by the local civil engineering company of Whittakers has closed one of the carriageways, leading to an early example of a 'contra-flow'. *R. T. Wilson*

Top With only six days to go before the Bristol Road route abandonment, car 620, built as an open-balconied tram by Brush in 1920, speeds along the central reservation towards the city from Rubery on the 71 route, having just left the Hole Lane stop. To the right, behind the trees, is the future site of Bournville Girls' Technical College, opened in October 1955. This tram was an all-electric car and was fitted with Dick, Kerr DK 301L 63hp motors. It had been transferred from Miller Street on Thursday 19 June and would go back to the north side of the city on the day before the closure. *P. Jaques*

Middle The rise out of the Griffins Brook valley was a steady, fairly slow climb for a fully laden 40hp four-wheeler. The 301 Class, the backbone for many years of both Bournbrook and Selly Oak depots' tram fleets, was displaced by the more powerful re-motored 512 and 587 Classes of bogie cars in 1939. Car 321, an open-balconied 1911-vintage tram, had been at Miller Street until March 1929, when it went to Selly Oak depot. It was transferred to Rosebery Street on 29 March 1939 and was later to become one of 50 of the class to be repainted during the Second World War in the drab grey livery. Here it is seen on the 72 route in the late 1930s at the Northfield end of the reserved track at Whitehill Lane. It is passing the then Royal Hospital for Crippled Children, which had formerly been a large private house known as Woodlands; this in turn became The Royal Orthopaedic Hospital. *Author's collection*

Bottom Car 734 enters the long section of reserved track at St Lawrence Road as it travels towards the city working the 70 route. This class of 30 EMB air-braked tramcars finished their 26 years in service working mainly from Selly Oak depot, although there was always the odd one or two allocated to Cotteridge. Car 734 looks as if the nearest platform has sagged a little under the strain of running at fairly high speed along Bristol Road's reserved track. This splendid reserved section was a highlight of the Birmingham system. *R. T. Wilson*

Opposite above The transfer of the 587 Class of Brush-built all-electric bogie cars to Selly Oak depot, after the closure of the Hockley and West Bromwich routes in April 1939, helped to maintain the service frequency on the busy south-western route along Bristol Road. All of the class were re-motored with Dick,

Kerr DK 30/1L 63hp motors in the late 1920s, which made them compatible with the 732 Class, fitted with EMB air-track brakes. Car 623 was a Selly Oak car almost continuously following the closure of Hockley, and is standing at the Bundy clock in Northfield on the section of street track on the city side of the shopping centre outside the early-20th-century premises of Daniel & Son when working the 71 route in early 1952. The last building in the distance with the tall chimneys is the Travellers Rest public house, which, rather incongruously, was built in the 1920s in a mock-Cotswold style surmounted with a thatched roof! *R. T. Wilson*

Below Strengthened 1913 Brush-built tram 517 leads 792, 15 years younger, across the traffic lights at the Bell Hotel junction, both working on the 70 route from the city. The extent of the body rebuilding can be seen on the older tram as the bulkhead window and the adjacent lower saloon ventilator were plated over with quarter-inch-thick steel plates. Also waiting at the traffic lights is an almost new Austin Devon A40 four-door saloon with a nearly new motorist, judging by the 'L' plates. The buildings behind the vehicles on the Church Road side of Bristol Road South were demolished in the early 1960s, but the replacement shops lay unfinished for many years. Eventually the Grosvenor shopping centre was completed, which today dominates this junction. *Author's collection*

Top In Birmingham, as in most large cities, directions are given by the location of notable landmarks such as crossroads, churches, important shops, but most commonly by the names of local public houses. Northfield had three of note on the main Bristol Road. Before the shopping centre on the city side was the aforementioned Travellers Rest. On the Longbridge side was the Black Horse, which was an excellent copy of a Tudor half-timbered manor house. In the

background here, in the midst of the shopping centre, is the Bell Hotel, a rather ornately gabled and towered Edwardian hostelry, standing on the corner of Bell Lane. At the time of the pub's construction, the old village of Northfield lay relatively undisturbed away from the main road route, which went to Bromsgrove, just over a mile away to the south-east; as a result the whole of the area retained its agricultural nature. In fact, for many years after its construction the land next door to the Bell was occupied by the barns and outhouses of a farm. Today the site is occupied by a much smaller, 1980s-built Bell public house and a McDonald's restaurant. On Saturday 7 June 1952 car 798 waits to leave the Northfield clocking-in point on its way to Navigation Street while working the 70 route. *R. F. Mack*

Middle Perhaps combining the best looks of the earlier totally enclosed trams with the technically advanced air-brake equipment of the later trams originally allocated to Washwood Heath and Cotteridge is one of the Brush/EMB 732 Class. Car 757, a 63hp car of 1926, stands outside the Bell Hotel on its way to Rednal in 1946, with the Church Road junction on the right. Church Road originally led directly to the old village centre of Northfield around the twin delights of the medieval St Laurence's Church and the Great Stone Inn, the latter dating from the early 18th century. Both Northfield and Selly Oak were, and are still today, notorious bottlenecks along the otherwise dual-carriageway Bristol Road and Bristol Road South. Various schemes have been planned and, in the case of Selly Oak, even implemented, but the traffic congestion in these two shopping areas, which over half a century ago were laid at the door of the trams, is proportionately worse! Car 757 is still wearing its pre-war livery, which by this date was beginning to look a little care-worn. *F. E. J. Ward*

Bottom The problems caused by picking up and setting down passengers without the benefit of kerb-side loading are very well demonstrated in this scene on the final Saturday morning in the centre of Northfield. Brush air-brake car 775 stands opposite the Bell Hotel, marooned by its own inflexibility in the middle of the road, while an Ansells brewery Leyland Comet is held up by the milling passengers. It is fortunate for the tram users that private car traffic in the early post-war years was so light. The traffic bottlenecks at Selly Oak and Northfield had attracted criticism from the 1920s, and the contributory role played by the trams was criticised even then. Car 775 was not used after the end of this day, but was stored on the central reservation of the Bristol Road for some 13 days before being driven away for scrapping at Witton. *R. Knibbs*

Above right The busy suburb of Northfield was surprisingly poorly covered by photographers, who seemed to prefer the outer termini of Bristol Road. However, here car 627 is caught crossing the turnback points used by the 69 route trams when they reached the splendidly turreted Bell Hotel. The tram is working on the 70 route and is travelling northwards towards the city in the summer of 1952. Just 18 months before this photograph was taken, Selly Oak depot had seven 587 Class trams numbered in the 620 sequence; of these, only car 627 survived the mass withdrawals of September 1950 and remained in regular use on the Bristol Road services. On the right, picking up passengers on the 71 route to Rubery is air-brake bogie car 743, carrying the popular '3-in-One Oil' advertisement. Yet again the stream of passengers in the roadway shows the disadvantages of the absence of kerb-side loading. *Lens of Sutton*

Below Near the site of old Toll House in Bristol Road South, which had been demolished immediately before the Great War, car 772 passes through Northfield shopping centre on 17 May 1952. This Brush-bodied 62-seater air-braked EMB Burnley maximum-traction-bogie car entered service in October 1928 and served on the Washwood Heath bow-collector routes until the evening of Saturday 30 September 1950. It survived until despatched to Kyotts Lake Works for storage and subsequent breaking-up at Witton depot in early August 1952. In happier days, car 772 is working on the 70 service to Rednal; passing the double frontage of Adams Bothers electrical stores and Pollington's furniture store, it is being followed by a large late-pre-war Austin 18. On the left, parked beneath the trees near the junction with Lockwood Road, is a late Morris Twelve Series II registered in Birmingham in August 1937. *F. Lloyd Jones*

Top With only a few days to go before the abandonment of the Bristol Road and Cotteridge routes on 5 July 1952, car 737, one of the Brush-built EMB air-brake bogie cars of 1926, travels into Northfield on the 71 route from Rednal. It has just passed the Black Horse public house on the corner of Frankley Beeches Road to the left of the double benches. The abandonment of the trams not only led to new replacement bus services but the alteration of others and the closure of the single-deck-operated 23 service, which used Frankley Beeches Road. The Austin A40 10cwt van is parked on one of the few garages along the early 1950s Bristol Road South selling fuel from the typical 1950s triangular Cleveland petrol pumps. *R. T. Wilson*

Middle The distinctive Black Horse public house was built to the design of C. E. Bateman in 1929 for Davenport's brewery. It was constructed in the form of a mock-Tudor manor house and hardly missed a trick in persuading the passer-by that it was genuine; today, despite its youth, it is a Grade II listed building. Car 764 is on its way to the city on the 70 route in April 1952. Parked next to the Black Horse is a Morris Series Y-type 10cwt van belonging to Bradfords, the large local baker based opposite West Bromwich Albion's Hawthorns football ground. Beyond the tram in the distance are two early examples of articulated lorries, the nearer one being a wartime Bedford OW type. The distant Frankley Beeches Road was used by the 18 and 23 bus routes at this time to serve the Allens Cross municipal housing estate. *F. N. Lloyd Jones*

Bottom Strengthened Brush-built car 549 climbs Pigeon House Hill, Bristol Road South, on 5 July 1952 when running from the Longbridge direction on the 69 route short-working to Northfield. Until the mid-1930s this section of Bristol Road South was still farmland, and the only settlements beyond Northfield were at Tessall, at the bottom of the hill, which consisted of a few houses around a crossroads, and Longbridge. Behind the tram, turning across the central reservation into South Road, is an early post-war Morris Series Y 10cwt van belonging to Royal Mail. Car 549 was one of only two trams in the fleet (the other being MRCW car 645) to display the balcony-dash advertisement 'Pond for Tools', which it carried for more than 16 years. This tram would not be broken up after the closure of the Bristol Road group of routes, but would see out another year's service at Miller Street. It was one of the last 23 to be scrapped during August 1953. *A. Yates*

Right In the summer of 1952 car 795, one of the 1928 totally enclosed 63hp trams built by Brush, approaches the Austin factory, just visible behind the large trees on the left of the central reservation. To the right can be seen the extension to the Austin West Works, which was being constructed by the newly formed British Motor Corporation. Car 795 was used in experiments by the EMB company to solve the problem of the slow wheel-brake auto-valve release mechanism. With Metropolitan Electric car 350, nicknamed 'Poppy', it was fitted with a simple and cheap cam-operated arrangement that allowed the air-wheel brake to be exhausted

mechanically when the air-track brake was applied, which improved the driver's control over the braking as compared to the rest of the 762 Class. Car 795 was made standard with the rest of the class in 1941. *R. F. Mack*

Below Car 750 crests the railway bridge over the Halesowen branch line on 7 June 1952. The Halesowen Railway, opened on 10 September 1883 as a joint venture between the Great Western and Midland companies, left the latter's main line at Longbridge and had intermediate stations at Rubery and Hunnington before connecting with the GWR's branch line at Halesowen. The line should have become an important southern access route around the growing industrial West Midlands area, but unfortunately the line, for all its potential usefulness, had

its Achilles' heel at Dowery Dell. Here a 660-foot-long cast-iron trestle viaduct took the line over a 100-foot-deep valley; a 10mph speed limit and a weight restriction severely limited the types of locomotives that could be used. Although it was later used to bring Austin car-workers to the Longbridge factory from the Black Country, the Halesowen line was never a success and was eventually closed on 6 January 1964; the station used by the Austin workers was to the west of the bridge seen here, and workmen's services, introduced as part of the First World War armaments drive, continued for another 40 years. Interestingly, this Longbridge station was never mentioned in any public timetable, despite having its booking and enquiry office staffed by British Railways officials. *H. B. Priestley*

Below The giant Austin Works at Longbridge needed 91 trams at peak periods to move the workforce at a time when Selly Oak depot's total complement of trams was rarely more than about 100. The tram service from Northfield was opened to Longbridge on 17 December 1923 as the 72 service, becoming the southern limit of the Bristol Road service for barely five months until a further section of central reservation track was built along Lickey Road to the city boundary as the 70 service to Rednal. In the left middle distance is the traffic island directly opposite the main entrance to the Austin factory, outside which the Vauxhall J 14/6 and Riley 1½-litre RMA on the right are parked. It was through the Bristol Road South island that the trams passed on their way to Rubery, which was the last reserved track reservation on Bristol Road to be opened as the 71 service on 8 February 1926. Car 754, on the right, was a Brush-bodied EMB air-brake car of 1926, an odd enclosed tramcar in the fleet, having been fitted experimentally in June 1931 with a removable window and an extra grab handle in order to allow easier access to the roof. It will advance over the points in front of it before reversing back to the shelters where car 623 stands loading up before leaving to go back to the city centre. Car 623 was destined to be the penultimate tram in the closing procession of the whole system on 4 July 1953; it is somewhat forgotten that it was also the last tram to arrive at Witton depot for scrapping from Miller Street, arriving at 8.15pm on Tuesday 7 July 1953. *T. J. Edgington*

Bottom The imposing iron shelters on the central reservation outside the Austin factory in Lickey Road were designed to accommodate the thousands of car-workers who swarmed on to the waiting trams at the end of each shift. Car 534 stands on the reserved track outside the factory on 3 June 1952 before leaving for the 70 terminus at Rednal. In 1905 Herbert Austin left the Wolseley Sheep Shearing Machine Company to set up his own car manufactory in derelict premises that had made colour-printed tin containers; opened in 1894 by Birmingham printers White & Pike, the company had hit financial difficulties in 1902 and vacated the site. Austin and his partners, Frank Keyser and Harvey Du Cros, purchased it on 10 November 1905 and built their factory on the south side of the Halesowen Railway branch line, and to the east side of Bristol Road South under which the railway passed. As early as July 1913 Birmingham Corporation had bought ten Daimler 40hp motor-buses to act as feeders to the Selly Oak tram route to take the Austin car-workers to the factory. Gradually the pull of this labour to Longbridge encouraged housing developments beyond Northfield towards the south-west. By the early 1920s the buses of the day were unable to cope with the increasing demands of the Austin works, so on 17 December 1923 the 72 service finally replaced them. *A. N. H. Glover*

Rednal

Top The climb from Longbridge up Lickey Road to the Rednal terminus was just over a mile long, and progressed from the industrial landscape at the bottom of the hill through a long horse-chestnut-lined central reservation, before reaching Cofton Park. The park was open farmland until it was made public in 1936; it was originally known as High Park. The parked Austin Seven Ruby is the only identifiable car in sight; it was made in the factory about half a mile away. Car 796 is working on the 70 route on 3 June 1952, and is passing Edgewood Road, having travelled one stop from the tram terminus at Rednal. This former village had become part of the city in 1911 and in contrast to the newly grown suburbia had a distinctly 'touristy' feel about it, as it catered for all the summer tram-borne day-trippers. This member of the 762 Class had been modified so that its EMB air-wheel and air-track brakes could be applied at the same time. This proved popular with the motormen, producing a jerk-free and more positive braking action, but was removed in August 1941 after nearly 11 years of service because it was non-standard. *A. N. H. Glover*

Middle Speeding away down the hill in Lickey Road is Brush-bodied air-brake EMB bogie car 755, which entered service in the early months of 1927. It has just left the Rednal terminus and is almost at the junction with Leach Green Lane. On a sunny summer's day in 1951 it is carrying an advertisement for Dreft, a successful soapless detergent that had only been introduced the previous year; it claimed to have '5 times more lather' than its competitors. This section of reserved track opened on 14 April 1924 to a stub terminus opposite the Hare & Hounds public house, and it would be another year before the famous loop was brought into use. Car 755 was eventually withdrawn early in March 1952 with defective trucks and was broken up at Witton depot during July. *Lacey's Studios*

Bottom On arrival at Rednal, the track crossed the carriageway at the top of the hill at Lickey Road opposite the Hare & Hounds and entered the 200-yard loop at the terminus. Car 528 is leaving the central reservation on a sunny day in the summer of 1951, and the driver is looking in his mirror for any vehicles that might be approaching, although it appears that the only car nearby, a 1937 Austin Ten, is stationary. Car 528 was one of the 67 of the 512 Class of 1913 to survive the Second World War. Of these, 25 had been re-motored in 1927 with GEC WT32R 70hp motors. All of the surviving 70hp cars were rewired and had their bodies strengthened in about 1948, and evidence for this can be seen here as the bulkhead window on the platform has been plated over. *S. J. Eades*

Above Rednal was the gateway to the 950-foot-high Lickey Hills, with rocks dating from the Silurian geological period and forming part of a ridge that goes from the Clent Hills in the south through the Lickeys and on to Sedgley, forming part of the main watershed in England. On high-days and holidays during the late 1920s and 1930s, the extra traffic generated by the attractions of the hills was phenomenal. The Bilbery tea-rooms, the Cofton Wood tea-rooms, country hostelries and public houses such as the Hare & Hounds at Rednal, fairgrounds, walks through the woods and in the hills, the landscaping of the River Arrow valley with waterfalls, wooden bridges and ornamental gardens, as well as the revered grave of Cardinal Newman near the Oratory Retreat House of 1854, were all attractions at the end of a fivepenny tram ride. On days such as these, Selly Oak had to bring in extra tramcars from other depots, although Moseley was the favoured supplier. Even as late as Easter 1948, 40 Class cars were supplementing the usual bogie cars. Here cars 446, 431 and 436 have just unloaded and will move around the terminus loop before heading back to the city. The second car, 431, still in pre-war livery, had a different top deck from the remaining members of the 401-450 Class, distinguishable by its lack of opening window ventilators. Car 431 was used as the 'Committee Car' as a single-decker from new. From 1916 until 1922 it was used as a tractor, with the unmotored ex-Company car 509, on the Nechells service, before receiving a new top deck in May 1923, built at Kyotts Lake Road Works. *R. Herbert*

Below The terminal loop was also used for stabling 18 trams as Selly Oak depot's allocation was more than its capacity. Car 788 is the last of the ten parked trams visible at the terminus, all with their trolleypoles tied down. The terminal loop was laid out on a grandiose scale to cater for the hundreds of passengers travelling to the 950-foot-high Lickey Hills for a cheap escape into the countryside. There they could enjoy the 'Brummies' playground, which had been donated initially by the generosity of the Cadbury family in 1906, with country walks through a mixture of open parkland and picturesque arboreal glades. The decline in this trade began with the increase in post-war car ownership – the pleasant walks in the countryside became less attractive when a coach trip to Weston-super-Mare or Rhyl came within the financial grasp of the pre-war visitors. That and the abandonment of the trams sounded the end for the Lickey Hills as a major day-trip attraction. *W. J. Wyse*

Opposite top With the leafless trees standing starkly against the sky above the impressive tram shelters at Rednal, car 344 stands empty on 6 January 1938 at the 70 route terminus. The shelters were constructed in 1925 at the same time as the loop line in order to cater for the large numbers of day-trippers. For a short time before this the terminus had been temporarily located near Leach Green Lane. The tram is one of

the 301 Class constructed by UEC in 1911, and, except for the later enclosed balconies on all the bogie cars built from car 637 onwards, this class set the design for all subsequent Birmingham tramcars. They were the first to have enclosed vestibules from new as well as having three-sided dash panels. This open-balcony, low-height, 52-seater tram was one of about 60 of the basically similar 301 and 361 Classes that were allocated to Selly Oak depot throughout the 1930s. The closure of the Dudley and West Bromwich routes at the beginning of April 1939 had enormous knock-on effects regarding tram allocation; a mass exodus of the four-wheelers occurred from Selly Oak, with car 344 leaving in May 1939. It was finally withdrawn in September 1950, being one of the last five four-wheelers to operate from Washwood Heath depot. *H. B. Priestley*

Middle In December 1944 grey-painted car 525 caught fire at the Rednal terminus, allegedly because of an electrical cable fault; although the body was gutted, the trucks and controllers were later salvaged for further use. Here the forlorn remains of the car stand where the fire took place on the loop. The grey livery, the headlight masks and the wartime white edgings to the fenders and the body have largely survived the conflagration, but the interior fittings and apparently every pane of glass have been totally destroyed. The remains went back to the car's home depot at Selly Oak, where they were stored for several months before being broken up in Sampson Road Paint Shop, the depository of a number of wartime tramcar casualties and also the 16 Nechells trolleybuses that had been withdrawn on 1 October 1940. *BCT*

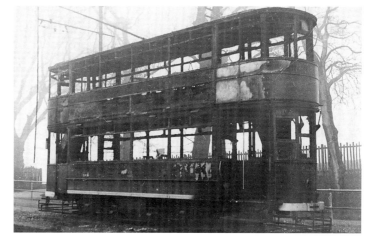

Bottom The Rednal terminus was like no other in Birmingham, with its large and carefully landscaped gardens within the purpose-built 200-yard-long loop. Car 802, one of the Brush-bodied EMB air-brake 63hp cars with the ungainly eight-windowed top-decks of 1928, stands at the exit of the Rednal terminus on 29 June 1952 alongside the advertisement proclaiming the 10pm departure of the last tram back to the city centre. *A. N. H. Glover*

Below Numerically the last of Moseley Road's allocation of half a dozen 301 Class trams, car 389 has just arrived at Rednal on the 709 route in the summer of 1949. In the background car 548 heads a line of trams waiting to leave the terminus. The short-trousered boys glance at the elderly, open-balconied tram, while the Inspector, holding a point bar in his right hand, looks at the track just in front of the tram. He was also employed to direct cars into the loop or the stub terminus as he deemed appropriate. In the summer months Moseley Road depot supplied extra trams to augment the normal service cars operated by Selly Oak depot. They would start at the Queen's Hotel end of Navigation Street and use the crossover into John Bright Street, which was only otherwise used for journeys to Kyotts Lake Road Works. At the end of the Lickey Hills summer season in 1949, that manoeuvre was discontinued, as the Moseley Road group of tram routes closed at the beginning of October. *P. Jaques*

Bottom On its way back to the city from Rubery, car 781 negotiates the traffic island at Longbridge junction outside the Austin factory. The two main routes diverged at this point; the 70 route to Rednal continued off the right-hand side of the photograph, while the 71 route followed the Rubery branch, which 781 is leaving. This tram, with just a hint of a sagging platform, is a 1928 EMB air-brake car built by Brush and is carrying the '3-In-One Oil' advertisement. This was on the balcony panels of well over 100 trams in the last few years of operation, having been introduced in July 1951. *W. J. Wyse*

Opposite top On a hot summer's day in July 1952, 60-seater Brush-built car 735 leaves the Rubery branch along Bristol Road South, emerging from the reserved island track before starting the climb over the railway bridge towards Northfield and the city. The row of utility-style Midland Red bus shelters just beyond the island to the left of the tram show that it was not just the Birmingham tram fleet that was required to move the Austin workers every day; Midland Red's service to Bromsgrove via Rubery village had a large part to play in the works services. The

carriageway and central reservation on Bristol Road South look much the same today as they did in 1952; it is the land use on either side of the road that has altered. Maisonettes were built in the late 1950s near the bus shelters, and the wooden-hut-style Longbridge Assembly Rooms opposite on the extreme right has been replaced by what is today a Rover Cars training school. The one major change from the 1950s is that the wide and spacious dual-carriageway, which was empty then, is still able to cope with the demands of the traffic of the 1990s, a testimony perhaps to the foresight of the town planners of the post-Great War period. *A. Yates*

Middle Picking up passengers at the Longbridge junction, with Bristol Road South and Lickey Road to the right, car 752 is working on the 71 service from Rubery on 12 April 1939. To the right are the office buildings of the Austin Motor Company, while over the distant bridge to the left of the tram is Longbridge railway station. The tramcar spent its first eight years of service at Rosebery Street depot and was transferred to Selly Oak in March 1934. This classic picture of a Birmingham tramcar in the inter-war period has all the facets of the BCT system, with tram stop signs, the tubular steel passenger barriers and the well-strung overhead wiring suspended from the delicately finialled traction poles. *H. B. Priestley*

Bottom Another view of the junction shows car 559 leaving Bristol Road South and passing the pumping station in the background. It is 3 June 1952 and this strengthened Brush-built car of 1913 would be one of the trams to survive the Bristol Road abandonment and be transferred to Miller Street depot for a further year's use on the remaining Aston Road routes. It is carrying the full post-war simplified livery, which although not as ornate as the lined-out pre-1946 style, did have a certain dignified charm, especially when the tram was in newly painted condition. Birmingham's trams always carried advertisements, although not every tram was so adorned. Car 559 carries some that would please the 1950s housewife: on the front balcony panels is the slogan that 'Bovril puts beef into you', while 'Tide – New Weekly Wash Sensation', a product introduced in October 1951, mops up the Bovril stains afterwards! *A. N. H. Glover*

Rubery

Top The rain glistens on the roofs of the interwar shops on the corner of Bristol Road South and Cliff Rock Road as totally enclosed EMB air-brake car 746 climbs up the gentle ascent from Longbridge towards the terminus of the 71 route at Rubery. The Rubery extension was the last to be completed as part of the Bristol Road extension and improvement schemes of the 1920s, opening on 8 February 1926. Only the route extensions to Short Heath, Pype Hayes, Hall Green, Stechford and Fort Dunlop would be built after this date, and all but the last used reserved track along arterial routeways. This early 1951 view shows that the tramway reservation was an integral part of the interwar thinking about town planning in Birmingham, being at the centre of a tree-lined 120-foot dual carriageway. Today, as the cars and buses queue in Bristol Road South having left the nearby M5 motorway and struggle in ever-increasing congestion towards Longbridge and Northfield, the wide grassed central strip stands in mute testimony to the concept of fast and economical high-speed trams on sleeper-laid, ballasted track. *W. J. Wyse*

Middle The last of the 732 Class cars, 761, approaches the last quarter-mile of the 71 route on the same miserable day as the previous photograph. This tram operated some 850,000 miles in its 26-year operating life. By way of comparison – albeit not quite fair as passenger loadings were then much higher – in 1970 West Midland PTE used more than 50 of the 3881-3980 Class of 33-foot-long Daimler Fleetline CRG6LXs on virtually the same routes. By 1981 all these buses had been withdrawn, mainly because their bodies were deteriorating so badly! *W. J. Wyse*

Bottom Standing at the Rubery terminus of the 71 route in the later days of the Second World War is car 551. It is fitted with masks on the headlights, and also visible is the small wartime rear light assembly mounted in a small box structure with the exposed wiring passing down behind the fender; this arrangement was altered to the more permanent Sanders lights fitted after the war. The tram also has the fenders painted white to make its edges more visible during the blackout, although with so little street and vehicle lighting available, the trams' near invisibility made little difference to other road users, who were also groping around in the darkness hoping to avoid other vehicles. Vehicle lighting restrictions were lifted in Birmingham on 6 January 1945. The tram also carries the uncommon, late-wartime advertisement 'Victory Will Be Sweeter With Mars'. Car 551 was experimentally fitted in July 1928 with a bow collector prior to their introduction on the Washwood Heath air-brake bogie cars. After the successful introduction of the

similarly equipped 762 Class, car 551 reverted to being fitted with the normal trolleypole and Boot design of trolley wheel. In January 1928 it was one of ten of the 512 Class to be fitted with the new design of top cover, which had an eight-window upper saloon to the same design as the contemporary 762 Class. *R. Elliott*

Top The Rubery terminus was just inside the Birmingham boundary near the north end of Leach Green Lane opposite the grounds of Rubery Hill Hospital. This was a considerable distance short of the Rose & Crown in Rubery, over the Worcestershire border, which had been used as a terminus by the Corporation's Daimler motorbuses to Rubery in 1914. The new tram terminus had to be partially excavated from the side of a sandstone hill and sufficient area was cleared for a terminal loop, which in the event was never built; many years later the wide open space was used for the fly-over of the Rubery By-Pass. Compared to the nearby Rednal terminus, the shelters at Rubery always appeared to be the poor relation, stuck in a no-man's-land well short of Rubery village. Brush-bodied EMB air-brake car 755 stands at the terminus on 15 September 1951. *A. K. Terry*

Middle The sight of lightweight car 842 working away from its normal Cotteridge haunts was unusual, but here it is being used on a Light Railway Transport League (LRTL) tour on Saturday 7 June 1952. It is waiting behind Brush air-brake car 752, which in turn waits for similar tram 744 to leave the single section of track adjacent to the Bundy clock. The comparison between the modern-looking 842 and the other two trams gives the impression that the nearer, traditional-looking trams belong to another generation of tramcar construction – in fact, cars 744 and 752 are only three years older! Despite the provision for a loop, the terminal stub at the end of the reserved track seemed adequate to cope with the tram traffic. *J. H. Meredith*

Bottom On the evening of that Saturday, 5 July 1952, tram 777 closed the Bristol Road route. It finally reached Selly Oak depot in the early hours of Sunday morning at about the same time as car 800 was becoming the last tram into Cotteridge depot. The closure of the Bristol Road service was marked by the Transport Department using a tram with a fairly memorable fleet number. Car 777, one of the former bow-collector trams allocated for so many years to Washwood Heath, ran a complete round trip from Navigation Street to Rednal before returning to the depot. By the next day, it and 53 other trams from Selly Oak and Cotteridge depots were parked on the central reservation near Eastern Road awaiting their next and final move to Witton, where they were broken up by W. T. Bird of Stratford-upon-Avon. *Author's collection*

PERSHORE ROAD AND COTTERIDGE

The Kings Norton and Northfield Urban District Council obtained the necessary powers to build an electric overhead tramway along Pershore Road to Cotteridge in 1901. The route of the new line was linked to the City of Birmingham Tramways Bristol Road route via Pebble Mill Road. As a result of this inevitable integration with the existing CBT system, the Urban District Council approached the tramway company to work the line to Cotteridge on its behalf.

The Birmingham boundary at that time was marked by Bournbrook, so that the quarter-mile section from Bristol Road along Pebble Mill Road to the bridge on Pershore Road opposite Cannon Hill Park was laid by Birmingham Corporation, as it was within its boundary, but at the expense of Kings Norton and Northfield UDC. The Corporation then let the line to the UDC for a nominal rent.

The Pershore Road service was opened between the stub terminus in Suffolk Street via Bristol Road and Pebble Mill Road as far as the temporary terminus near Mayfield Road, Stirchley, on 20 May 1904, although the CBT trams displayed the destination of Breedon Cross. The line was extended to Cotteridge on 23 June 1904. During this five-week period the new service was operated from Bournbrook depot.

The CBT open-top cars used on the route were from the 189-192, 193-208, 209-216 and 239-242 Classes, although other cars, including the converted bogie cars 181-188 were undoubtedly used at Cotteridge depot. After it was opened in late June 1904 with an allocation of just eight trams, Cotteridge was regarded by the CBT Company as just an outstation for Bournbrook depot. There was a considerable amount of interchange of rolling-stock between the two depots as there was no separate allocation of tramcars. Rather surprisingly this situation continued throughout the years of Corporation operation, which accounts for the regular appearance of odd Selly Oak cars at Cotteridge depot and vice versa.

CBT's 21-year lease on the operation of the Bristol Road route was due to expire in 1911, and the Pershore Road lease was to expire on the same date. The electrification agreement of 21 July 1900 allowed for Birmingham Corporation to purchase all the tram rolling-stock, electrical feeders and overhead within the city boundary on 1 July 1911; it duly took over on that date, at first on behalf of Kings Norton, until on 9 November 1911 Kings Norton Urban District, together with Aston Manor, Erdington, Handsworth, Northfield and Yardley, became part of Greater Birmingham.

The Pershore Road route and Cotteridge depot thereupon became solely owned by BCT. Thus it was that some 20 trams were transferred to BCT in July 1911, and a further 41 were similarly taken over with the purchase of the remainder of the CBT system at the end of the year.

On the Pershore Road route, as operated by both CBT and the Corporation, trams left Bristol Road via Pebble Mill Road. This was originally a narrow road through open land, but in 1919 it was to become something of a trail-blazer as it was selected to be rebuilt as the prototype of the new arterial road system in the city with a central reservation capable of carrying tramcars.

At the junction with Pershore Road opposite Cannon Hill Park, the trams turned right and crossed the old city boundary at the Bournbrook bridge and into Selly Park. From here the tram route followed Pershore Road to the terminus at Cotteridge.

The gentle climb through Selly Park passed initially through a residential area of late-19th-century housing, although opposite Kensington Road there were a few attractive terraced houses from the early 1840s. On reaching Kitchener Road the route turned slightly south-westwards and continued past a long row of large, distinctive early-20th-century terraced housing.

The former hamlet of Ten Acres was

reached about 1¼ miles from Pebble Mill Road. After the track was doubled in 1914, Ten Acres became the first main turnback point along the route; in later years this became the short-working from the city, numbered 53. Ten Acres was at the junction with Dogpool Lane, and beyond this was a section of single track about a quarter of a mile long with a passing loop. This narrow piece of roadway had houses and industry on either side; historically it had its origins in the industrial mills associated with the nearby Griffins Brook and the River Rea.

Once Griffins Brook had been crossed, the route arrived at Stirchley. Here the route split, only the outward line continuing along Pershore Road. The inward route followed Hazelwell Street from the bifurcation opposite the British Oak at the rather solid-looking, turn-of-the-century Church of the Ascension northwards past the bottom on Bournville Lane, on the corner of which was the swimming baths and the library. On the east side, opposite Bournville Lane, was the original site of George Cadbury's first Day Release College, opened in the 1890s. After curving to the right Pershore Road was regained at Umberslade Road just short of the Three Horseshoes public house and outside the departmental store and headquarters of the Ten Acres & Stirchley Co-operative Society.

Immediately after the two sections rejoined at the British Oak public house, the busy Victorian suburban shopping centre of Stirchley Street was reached. At the far end of these shops, for the first six weeks of the line's operation, was the temporary terminus of Breedon Cross, which was actually some distance away, north of Fordhouse Lane.

Beyond the end of this straight quarter-mile-long section of street track, the route climbed and twisted sharply over Breedon Cross bridge. This took the tram tracks over the Worcester & Birmingham Canal and a little-used railway line, to reach the Breedon Cross public house, which dominated the southbound exit from the bridge, and past the Savoy cinema. The line then resumed its steady climb towards Cotteridge, ascending a short hill to Frances Road, passing Cotteridge School on the right, and rows of better-quality Victorian terraces on the left.

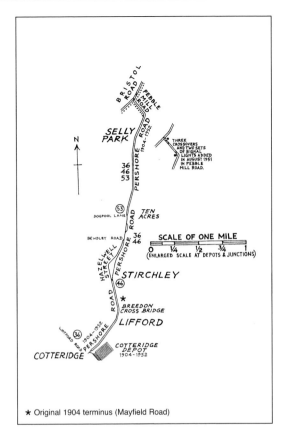

The Pershore Road and Cotteridge routes.

The final quarter-mile took the route past more late-19th-century houses and shops as well as crossing two railway bridges before curving away through the Edwardian shopping centre of Cotteridge, dominated by St Agnes's Church. At the far end of the shops, at Watford Road, the terminus was finally reached opposite Cotteridge depot, access to which was from the single terminal stub line.

The 36 route to Cotteridge allowed for a certain amount of high-speed running, and after the First World War bogie cars were the normal type on the route. In later years the newest of the traditional-looking Birmingham trams, the 812 Class of M&T bogie cars, were always associated with the service along Pershore Road. Added to the route's regular trams were the two lightweight cars, 842 and 843, the last trams purchased by the Corporation. After 1930 the depot allocation at Cotteridge remained remarkably stable.

Navigation Street to Pebble Mill Road

Below In common with those along Bristol Road, the Pershore Road tram route began at the heavily-canopied shelters in Navigation Street, where car 817, still in its pre-war livery, waits to leave for Cotteridge in the spring of 1947. This Short-bodied 63hp tram, mounted on Maley & Taunton bogies and equipped with separate air-wheel brake control, with air-track and magnetic braking available through the main controller, was the 'last word' in the development of the Standard Birmingham tramcar. The 30 trams of the 812 Class were delivered to Cotteridge depot between November 1928 and April 1929 to replace the motley collection of tramcars operating the 36 service along Pershore Road; most were still at work at the closure of the route 24 years later. However, car 817 would just fail to see out its time to the abandonment of 5 July 1952, having been sent to the works because of loose tyres. Queuing behind 817 is car

554, in the 1946 livery and working on the 33 route to Ladywood, a service that would be discontinued on 30 August 1947. Towering above the trams is the Central Technical College of 1893, employing a very rich red brick and terracotta decorative panels with elaborately carved windows and mullions. *W. A. Camwell*

Bottom The route used the loop around Navigation Street and John Bright Street, which had been introduced on 4 February 1902 for the CBT's electric trams working on Bristol Road to Bournbrook; this was some nine months after the route had been converted from the unreliable battery-accumulator tramcars on 14 May 1901, and the loop replaced the terminal stub in Suffolk Street and enabled the electric cars to get a little nearer to the centre of Birmingham without the awkward manoeuvres involved in reversing. Cars 826, 623, 605 and 812 stand in Navigation Street just above the loading shelters on 3 June 1950. Cars 826 and 812 were built by Short Brothers Ltd of Rochester, Kent, mounted on standard Brush underframes, and were associated almost exclusively with

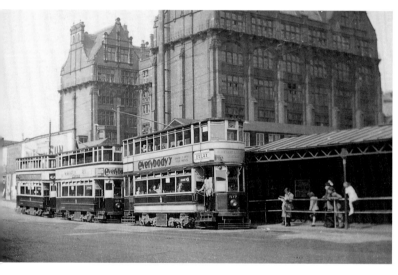

the Pershore Road route; this pair worked right up until the last day of Cotteridge operation. Brush-built car 623 was destined to be one of the two cars that finally closed the Birmingham system. Identical tram 605 was not so fortunate, being one of 26 of the 587 Class to be withdrawn when the EMB air-brake members of the 762 Class were transferred to Selly Oak depot upon the closure of the Washwood Heath routes on 30 September 1950. Car 605 was broken up at Witton by December of that year. *J. H. Meredith*

Opposite top The unique experimental Short Brothers-bodied lightweight tram 842 stands at the Navigation Street loading shelters working on the 36 route in June 1949. It was constructed using parts provided by Aluminium (TI) Ltd, Shorts and the Transport Department, who shared the development and construction costs of the vehicle over and above the normal price for a compositely constructed Birmingham Corporation tramcar, and entered service on 28 November 1929. With its domed roof, flush sides and four-bay construction, it was the most radically different-looking tramcar to enter service in the city. It was also fitted with English Electric lightweight steel bogies, which had 26-inch-diameter driving wheels and 20-inch-diameter pony wheels. This was one of the main reasons why it was the lowest top-covered tram in the BCT fleet, at 15ft 6in. In this picture it is still fitted with its original bogies,

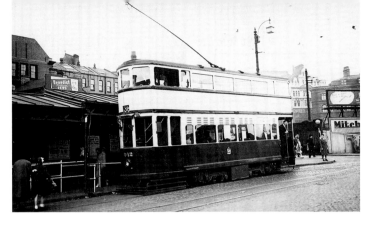

which were replaced by the Maley & Taunton ones from withdrawn car 821 in November 1950. One of the hoardings in the tram shelter announces that the West End cinema is showing *The History of Mr Polly*, starring John Mills in a 1949 adaptation of H. G. Wells's novel. *R. Marshall*

Middle A little girl looks on with interest from the window beneath the side destination box as three women alight from car 820 at the Horse Fair unloading island, working the 36 route on 21 June 1952. This island was removed just one week before the abandonment of the tram services so that the replacement buses would not be obstructed. Before the start of the construction of Smallbrook Queensway on 8 March 1957, Horse Fair and the nearby small-scale shopping area of Smallbrook Street were far more accessible for pedestrians; Smallbrook Street also allowed access to the markets area and New Street Station. However, this was all before the car boom and the consequent decline of public transport as a prime mover of people. The Singer Bantam car in the distance is the only other vehicle on an otherwise deserted city centre street, but within a few years it was deemed necessary to rebuild the street system as the exiting road pattern was becoming congested and unable to cope with the increase in car ownership. Consequently the urban landscape and road systems inherited from the late-Victorian growth of the city were lost. Car 820 was the only one of the Short Brothers-bodied Maley & Taunton air-brake cars to be strengthened; it re-entered service in November 1950 having had its bulkhead windows plated over in the same way as some 56 older trams. This modification can clearly be seen above the head of the first woman leaving the tramcar. *J. E. Cull*

Bottom When only about ten years old, car 830, built in 1928 and painted in the lined-out pre-war livery, takes the curve from Horse Fair into Bristol Street on its way out of the city on the 36 route to Cotteridge circa 1938. The width of Horse Fair reflects its former use as an occasional market place, the last horse fair having been held here in 1911. The buildings to the right of the tram are still there today, including the White Lion public house with its clock tower on the corner of Thorp Street, popular with theatre-goers attending performances at the nearby Birmingham Hippodrome. All the buildings on the left, including St Catherine of Sienna Roman Catholic church, the nearby school and the two small thoroughfares of Windmill Street and Little Bow Street, have all been swept away. Car 830 would later become one of the most photographed of all Birmingham's trams, when, with open balcony four-wheeler car 367, it toured what was left of the Birmingham system on 10 July 1949. *Author's collection*

Top There has been very little change in the character of Horse Fair between the previous pre-war picture and the early part of 1952, when similar Maley & Taunton air-brake car 815 is seen a few yards further on, travelling towards the city. It is about to pass some roadworks, an obvious hazard to other traffic but not, it seems, to the tram service; the temporary warning oil-lamps can be seen between the tramcar and the Morris Oxford taxi that has just turned out of Essex Street. To the left of the tram is a 'Tramway Repairs Keep Left' sign, warning other traffic of the obstruction in the carriageway. Car 815 worked on the 5½-mile Cotteridge route for almost all of its 24 years in service, amassing just over 700,000 miles. Its side panel carries an advertisement for Capstan cigarettes; tobacco advertising today is a controversial subject, but it was quite unusual for Birmingham tramcars to advertise cigarettes – in nearly 50 years of operation only three such advertisements were carried: for K4 cigarettes in the 1930s (see page 18), and Martin's Gold Leaf and Capstan between 1951 and 1953.

The M&T cars represented the last of the traditional style of Birmingham tram. Although new rocker-panelled trams were, by 1928, becoming rather outmoded, beneath the surface these BCT tramcars represented some of the most up-to-date technology in air-brake design. They featured an independent air-wheel brake to all eight wheels as well as an air-track brake, providing much smoother and more controllable braking compared with the previous EMB Class. These 16¾-ton cars were regarded as very 'sure footed' and provided the Cotteridge route with the most up-to-date trams in the Birmingham fleet. *R. T. Wilson*

Middle The 'palm tree' advertisement on the wall above the shoe-repairers near the corner of Sun Street is something of a climatic non sequitur on this damp Saturday, 21 June 1952, just two weeks before the closure of the Cotteridge and Bristol Road routes. The traffic-light-controlled junction in Bristol Street, over which Short Brothers-bodied car 829 is passing, was the crossing point of the number 8 Inner Circle bus route. Most of Bristol Street was tree-lined and was a dignified, if somewhat run-down, approach from the south-west by the main A38 road into the city. Today this junction does not exist, and all the buildings in the background were swept away in the Lee Bank comprehensive redevelopment of the area immediately to the north-west of Bristol Street at the end of the 1950s. Not only were high-rise flats built upon the site of the shops, but Bristol Street itself was widened into a four-lane dual carriageway as part of the 1970s Middle Ring Road scheme, creating an underpass section linking the former Belgrave Road with Lee Bank. *J. E. Cull*

Opposite bottom Cotteridge depot's normal allocation of tramcars consisted of all 30 of the 812 Class together with the two lightweight trams 842 and 843. It did, however, draw upon the allocation of Selly Oak for up to four or five extra trams from about 1950. The first type of air-brake car, the Brush-bodied EMB cars of the 732 Class, were favoured in these temporary transfers; they could easily be recognised as they were of four-bay construction, while Cotteridge's regular allocation of the totally enclosed 812 Class had the eight-windowed upper saloon common to all the later standard air-brake bogie cars. A further distinguishing feature, which car 750 clearly shows, was the fitting of the cleaners' balcony grab rails on the underside of the roof adjacent to the destination number blind. Car 750 was first used by Cotteridge in April 1950 and remained there until September 1951, which therefore dates this view to within that 17-month period. The tram is seen in Bristol Road approaching Speedwell Road at an architecturally interesting point in the housing development along this route. The housing up to Pebble Mill Road was generally Victorian or Edwardian, and this was the first point where inter-war infilling had taken place, as shown by the white-painted 1930s-vintage house behind the post box. *C. Carter*

Top right The major alterations that have affected Bristol Road have been at the major road junctions. Car 763 rumbles across the traffic lights at the Priory Road intersection with Bristol Road; the large house on the corner is Greenmore College, a private school.

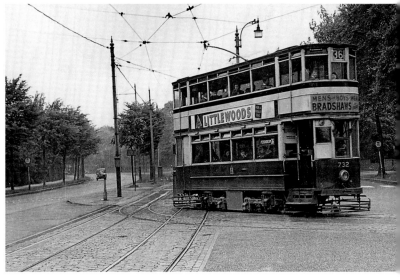

The tram is working the 36 route to Cotteridge in the early spring of 1952, and is travelling towards Pebble Mill Road. Car 763 was allocated to Cotteridge depot for just under two months from March 1952. Approaching the city is one of Midland Red's BMMO D5B types, among the last double-decker buses to be bodied by Brush of Loughborough between 1950 and 1952, when the firm stopped body manufacturing. This type remained in service until the mid-1960s, and just as Brush-built tram 763 belongs to the last generation of standard Birmingham tramcars, so the bus represents the last of the traditional heavyweight Midland Red double-deckers. *R. T. Wilson*

Above right The first member of the 30-strong 732 Class turns into Pebble Mill Road from Bristol Road on the 36 route to Cotteridge in June 1952. The condition of the track by this time had deteriorated from its pristine state in the inter-war years, as can be seen in the foreground – only essential track repairs were undertaken once the decision to abandon the routes was taken. Gradually tram-rides became more akin to endurance tests for intrepid travellers experiencing a fast journey along the reserved track to Rednal or Rubery, although on the more leisurely run to Cotteridge minor track deformities were less important. These lower-numbered examples of the first class of air-brake cars purchased in 1926 led reasonably quiet lives working mainly from Rosebery Street depot, where they were used on the fairly short 33 route to Ladywood. The day after Rosebery Street closed on Saturday 30 August 1947, the 11 trams of the 732 Class remaining there were moved to Selly Oak. Their excellent condition was soon put to the test on the high-speed Bristol Road routes, but they were used from time to time along Pershore Road to augment Cotteridge depot's fleet, as shown here. *R. Brook*

Below Cotteridge-based Short Brothers car 823 has just reached the junction with Bristol Road, having come up the slight rise on the reserved track of Pebble Mill Road; it will turn right across the southbound carriageway of Bristol Road before reaching the passenger shelter and Bundy clocks, which were shared with the Rednal and Rubery tram routes. Today the large gabled house looks out over the deserted grassed-over central reservation, and very few visitors to the city would ever realise that this had ever been a busy tram junction. The design details of these last traditional 812 Class Birmingham trams can be appreciated in this view. Their bodies continued the style of the previous 762 batch, in that the upper saloons were equipped with eight small windows between the bulkheads, enabling each row of passengers to control their own ventilation. Below the staircase at one end, beneath the lower saloon waistrail, are the ventilation louvres that were intended to prevent the rheostats from overheating; these are visible just to the right of the central reservation bollard, and were fitted to the complete class of 30 trams after 1937. Maley & Taunton provided the Burnley-style maximum traction bogies, which broke the pattern of the previous five orders that had all gone to EMB of Eagle Works, Moor Street, West Bromwich. The M&T design could be distinguished by the slightly squarer-topped axle-boxes. *R. Brook*

Bottom Travelling towards Cotteridge, the Pershore Road trams turned left into Pebble Mill Road within a few hundred yards of gaining the reserved track in Bristol Road. Pebble Mill Road was the shortest link between the latter and Pershore Road, and was used because Kings Norton UDC wished to gain access to the existing CBT lines on nearby Bristol Road. The Calthorpe family owned most of the land in the Edgbaston area and prohibited the building of anything to do with industry or commerce on it, although from about the 1860s they had to admit ordinary families. The houses built for these better-paid artisans were confined to the eastern and northern parts nearest to the inner areas of Birmingham. For the remainder, some of the best-known industrialists associated with the growth of Birmingham, the Cadbury, Chamberlain, Martineau, Ryland and Sturge families, all lived on the Calthorpe estate. As a direct consequence, the protectionist measures

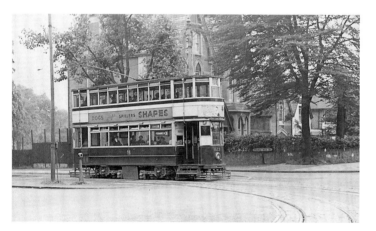

to ensure the dignity of the area affected things as mundane as ensuring that trees were planted and that services such as shops were kept to the minimum, and then only on the periphery of the estate. Even tram routes through the 'well-heeled' estate became a point of issue. The first section of dual carriageway in the city was built immediately prior to the First World War in Oxhill Road, Handsworth, but Pebble Mill Road was the first such road designed with a central reserved tram track. Described as a 'specimen road', it opened in 1919 and acted as a model for the main arterial routes such as Bristol Road, Tyburn Road and Stratford Road. *C. Carter*

Pebble Mill Road to Cotteridge

Top From Monday 3 September 1951 until the abandonment of the Bristol Road and Cotteridge routes on 5 July 1952, Pebble Mill Road was used for parking trams. This was because of the lack of space in Selly Oak depot while its ten tracks were converted for bus operation. As a result, two new crossovers were built in August 1951 so that the inbound track could be used for parking up to about 20 trams, while the resultant single outbound line for the length of Pebble Mill Road was protected at both ends by traffic lights, activated by skates on the overhead. Car 828 leaves the single-line section, passing the tram signal light and the wooden hut used by the BCT watchman during the depot conversion period. On the inbound line is the usual line of parked Selly Oak trams, the one car visible being 782. A third overhead wire has been provided so that service cars on their own wires could pass the parked trams without the need for any de-poling. *R. Brook*

Middle Brush-bodied EMB air-brake car 788 is at the rear of a row of tightly packed, parked Selly Oak-allocated trams. Only the fifth tram in the line belongs to one of the earlier classes, distinguishable by having four windows between the bulkheads rather than the eight of the later 762 Class. Behind the trams is open land that for many years was occupied by a riding school; an abiding memory of this site is of a succession of grey horses that seemed fascinated by the passing traffic! Today the land is occupied by the BBC's Pebble Mill Studio complex and the roadway is usually lined with parked cars overflowing from its car park. *R. T. Wilson*

Bottom The distant Ford Anglia disappears along the trackless Pershore Road, alongside Cannon Hill Park, while tram 813 prepares to leave the reserved track on Pebble Mill Road and turn right into Pershore Road. The layout of the overhead can be clearly seen; the extra wires coming from near the top of the traction pole fed current into the overhead at intervals along every route. The photographer, Ray Wilson, is standing on the River Rea bridge, which until 1911 was the boundary between Birmingham and Kings Norton. The group of children and the man carrying his young daughter are waiting for a city-bound tram at the oblong, red compulsory tram stop, perhaps after a visit to Cannon Hill Park. This 80-acre park was another site donated to Birmingham by Miss L. A. Ryland, and was opened to the public on 1 September 1873. If the Lickey Hills at Rednal were the day-trippers' resort at the edge of the city, Cannon Hill Park was large enough to be a lung of green space within the city that would attract people looking for less arduous arboreal walks. It was also served by the 37 tram route, which went to Willows Road via Balsall Heath. *R. T. Wilson*

Top Having turned from Pebble Mill Road into Pershore Road on its journey out of town, car 837 is about to cross the Bourn Brook, a small tributary of the River Rea, which it joined in the nearby Cannon Hill Park. The queue of intending passengers on the opposite side of the road appear to have had a day out in the park, but it looks as if they are in for a long wait! Car 837, a Short-bodied, totally enclosed EMB bogie tramcar, has left the only section of reserved track on the 36 route and will make a fairly leisurely run through Selly Park and on to Stirchley and Cotteridge. *R. T. Wilson*

Middle This circa 1916 view probably shows car 362, one of the 1912 UEC-built open-balcony trams mounted on UEC 7ft 6in trucks; it is passing First Avenue as it travels along Pershore Road in Selly Park. At that time these four-wheelers would have had only a few years left before being displaced by the 512 Class bogie trams that would serve the Cotteridge route until displaced in turn by the arrival of the air-brake 812 cars of 1929. The condition of the road surface is of interest: the Corporation Tramways Department was responsible for its tramlines and 18 inches on either side of the tracks, and until the 1930s quite often the remainder of the surface, as shown here, was of inferior quality. Stories of cars and bicycles getting their spindly tyres caught in the lines were thus quite often true, as the only reasonable road surface over which they could travel was on the properly maintained tram tracks. *Commercial postcard*

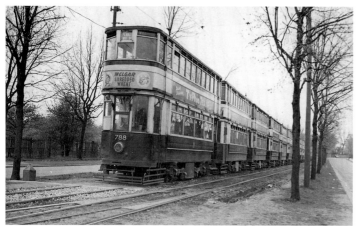

Bottom Car 189, a 50-seat open-top double-decker, was the first of four Brush-built trams built for Sheerness Tramways in 1902 as part of a batch of 12, and re-entered service with CBT in early 1904 wearing the still fresh Sheerness livery of chocolate and cream. These trams were allocated to Bournbrook depot, but in reality car 189 was allocated at various times to Cotteridge. It is travelling into Birmingham on the Pershore Road and entering the loop near Second Avenue, Selly Park, in about 1905. The only other vehicular traffic on the well-maintained road is a four-wheel cart, which demonstrates just how revolutionary was the introduction of the electric tramcar. Tram 189 was transferred to the parent Birmingham & Midland Joint Committee premises on 3 August 1911, then its fate is unclear; it was either sold to Devonport & District or entered service locally

with the local Dudley, Stourbridge & District Electric Traction Company. *Author's collection*

Right Car 839 approaches Kitchener Road on the Selly Park section of Pershore Road on Saturday 5 July 1952. Normal services were maintained throughout this last day of operation and the only things that distinguished it from any other Saturday were the notices pasted on the upper saloon balcony windows and tram stops temporarily affixed to the replacement bus stop posts. The following day car 839 would be placed in store on the Bristol Road central reservation near Eastern Road, then on Friday 11 July it would be driven across the city, together with seven others, to Witton depot where it would be broken up by W. T. Bird. Views of trams on this section of Pershore Road are very uncommon. On this curve there was a 'tram pinch' traffic sign warning other road users that the tram tracks crossed to the east side of the carriageway for about 20 yards and took a different line from the curve of the road; the two tracks can be seen in the foreground some distance away from the nearside kerb. The urban landscape here has hardly changed in the intervening decades, yet the whole ambience of this scene is redolent of another time, when public transport was a major facet of city life and the city's tramcars were the prime mover of people for work and leisure. *A. K. Terry*

Below On its way into the city in about 1947, car 830 is working on the 36 service from Cotteridge and has just pulled away from the Dogpool Lane tram stop, which was almost outside the gates of Selly Park School in Pershore Road. On the right is the long row of turn-of-the 20th-century houses that have always been known as the 'ABC houses', as they are named alphabetically from the Hobson Road end to the last house nearly opposite the tram. Their name plaques can just be seen between the first-floor windows; they went from ASTLEY to JARROW before the letters in the alphabet beat the number of houses. *R. Herbert*

Below The Dogpool Inn stood on the corner of Dogpool Lane and Pershore Road at Ten Acres. This garish self-advertising hostelry was the original public house at this crossroads, but despite all its immodest and boastful self-proclamation, it was demolished at the end of the 1920s and replaced by a Birmingham Municipal Bank. The pub on the opposite corner at St Stephens Road, the Ten Acres Tavern, was also pulled down. The replacement for both was built on the site of the Ten Acres Tavern but was confusingly named the Dogpool! It is now know as The Hibernian. The tramcar appears to be either car 323 or 353 of the 301 Class of four-wheel UEC open-balcony cars that replaced the ex-CBT trams on the Cotteridge route. It is seen in about 1913, and displays the flop-over destination boards used on Birmingham tramcars from 1909 until about 1920, when they were replaced by the more familiar small, square route number boxes. It is carrying an advertisement proclaiming that the Great Western Railway has the shortest route to London, which also dates the photograph to the years immediately prior to the First World War, as the GWR opened its Bicester 'cut-off' line through Aynho for passenger services between Birmingham Snow Hill and London on 1 July 1910. *Author's collection*

Bottom The first member of the Short Brothers class of 1928 stands at the Ten Acres junction with Dogpool Lane on its way to Cotteridge, in approximately the same position as the tram seen above. It is opposite Selly Park School, with the tall nave of Selly Park Baptist church visible on the left. There appears to be a delay, as the man standing in the road next to the tram is in conversation with the couple on the pavement – a photograph is a 1/25th-of-a-second moment in time, so what happened next must be open to conjecture. One hopes that the approaching Austin 10 will stop, or the man will make up his mind and board the 36 service tram. This 1952 view shows the extent of the straight run that the cars made from the distant bend at Kitchener Road past the long row of the 'ABC' terraced houses on the right. *R. Brook*

Opposite top A horse-drawn delivery van crosses Pershore Road and trots into Dogpool Lane opposite Ten Acres Post Office one summer's day in 1952. The early post-war MG Magnette four-door saloon is parked on the wrong side of the road outside Adams's tobacconist and confectionery shop as the shadow cast by the 16¾-ton tramcar passes across it. This section of the Pershore Road route marked the change from the large Victorian/Edwardian terraced housing of Selly Park to the mid-19th-century mixed residential and industrial land use associated

with the Ten Acres area of Stirchley. This settlement grew up around the nearby Dogpool Mill, which as well as being an iron-forge was also at a crossing point of the River Rea. The wide former turnpike route of Pershore Road narrowed at this small hamlet, and the tram tracks were reduced to a single line from this junction to Cartland Road. Car 816 is waiting for the approaching city-bound tramcar to leave the single line before itself negotiating the narrow quarter-mile section with its one passing loop. *Lens of Sutton*

Middle The strangely shaped towers of the Dogpool public house stand out above car 828 in the spring of 1952 as it comes towards the northern end of the single line near the Mitchells & Butlers advertisement for its 'Export' brand of bottled light ale. This tram, one of the Maley & Taunton air-brake cars constructed by Short Brothers in 1928, is on its way to the city terminus in Navigation Street, some 5½ miles away, and is approaching the outbound turnback point of the 53 route, which was a short-working of the main 36 service. The Dogpool passing loop was used by trams going to Cotteridge in order that city-bound trams could clear the next narrow section of line. *R. Brook*

Bottom The 29 cars of the 812-841 Class that survived the Second World War were all repainted into the post-war standard livery between September 1946 and September 1949. Car 817, working the 36 route and seen on the Dogpool loop from the other side of the road in about 1948, is still adorned in the pre-war livery with cream rocker-panels, lined-out paintwork and ornate-style fleet numbers. It was the penultimate member of the class to receive the post-war livery in March 1949, with only car 839 surviving longer in the old style of paintwork. Car 817 was also one of 25 members of the 812-841 Class to be reseated with 'in-line' instead of staggered upholstered tilting seats in the last four years before the Second World War. As a result its new seating capacity of 27 in the lower saloon and 33 in the upper was reduced by two. It was also one of the first four of the class to be experimentally fitted with external louvres in the dash panels to overcome the constant problem of heating rheostats. This modification was done in the spring of 1937, and was so successful that the remainder of the class

were similarly modified. Car 817 did not quite see out its full potential lifespan, being withdrawn in late May 1952 because of loose tyres, which, at that late stage, were not considered worth replacing. It was sent to Witton depot and was among the first cars after the Bristol/Pershore Road abandonment to be broken up by W. T. Bird & Son early in July 1952. *R. Herbert*

Above Car 839 approaches Stirchley, having left behind the distant towers of the Dogpool public house. This end of the single-line section was characterised on the eastern side by rows of small cottage-style terraced Victorian housing dating from the 1860s. These opened straight on to the pavement and their proximity to the noisy passage of the trams in the narrow roadway may have been a source of great irritation to their occupants. Later Victorian town planning attempted to avoid, where possible, the mistakes of earlier generations in that residential areas were segregated from industrial ones. Here in Stirchley the development of small industrial premises opposite the housing was a consequence of the industrial growth of the late 18th and early 19th centuries. This generally occurred where small streams were crossed by main routeways, in this case Griffins Brook, which flowed into the nearby River Rea, and the water supply was harnessed by water mills to provide power. The small enclave of metal-based industries opposite the houses in the Ten Acres area along Pershore Road was an early 20th-century relocation of the previous industrial site that included Dogpool Mill, which was an iron-rolling mill. The juxtaposition of housing and industry produced an area that always looked in need of renovation; it is surprising, therefore, that most of the buildings seen here in 1952 still remain occupied. *R. Brook*

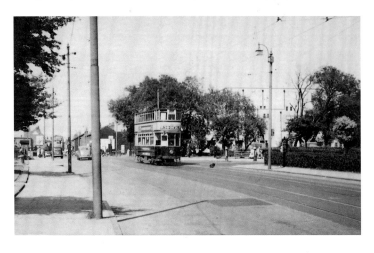

Below Beyond the Warwards Lane junction with Pershore Road lay the bridge over Bourne Brook and the adjacent Cartland Road. On this corner was the Pavilion Cinema opened on 28 November 1931 and architecturally and culturally a product of the 1930s; its gaunt white-pillared frontage can be seen between the trees to the right of car 830, working the 36 service during the last few days of operation in July 1952. This 63 hp tram, powered by two English Electric DK30/1 motors and mounted on Maley & Taunton Burnley maximum-traction bogies, entered service in late 1920 and spent all its working life giving trouble-free service to the residents of Pershore Road – at least one member of the 812 Class only ever visited Kyotts Lake Road Works for repainting and normal overhauls and never needed anything other than routine maintenance. *A. K. Terry*

Above The approaching Short Brothers tramcar, 839, is about to enter the one-way system in Stirchley. Southbound trams took the line to the right into Pershore Road while those going to the city terminus emerged from the track on the left from Hazelwell Street. The tram is approaching the Three Horseshoes public house, which stands on the corner of Umberslade Road. Opposite, a 1934 Birmingham-registered Morris Ten is parked outside Dewhurst's butchers shop. The disappearing Midland Red double-decker working the 147 route from Redditch is a Brush-bodied BMMO D5B of 1951. This view of Stirchley, taken on 7 June 1952, shows another section of the Cotteridge route that has hardly altered in the intervening years. *H. B. Priestley*

Below On the last day of operation, Saturday 5 July 1952, car 816 works its way beyond Stirchley Baths, built in 1911,

and on towards the large out-of-town Ten Acres & Stirchley Co-operative Society store and headquarters, which was demolished in the mid-1970s and replaced by a large Co-op supermarket. The houses and cottages, the latter dating from the 1840s, have long since disappeared to be replaced by discount warehouses, but the houses on the right and the one-way system in Hazelwell Street still remain. The tram clearly shows the small Sanders rear lamp to the right of the headlight; this replaced the temporary rear light fitted for blackout conditions, which was mounted in a small box-like structure just above the fender and at least gave motorists at night some indication of where the rear of the tram was in relation to the front of the car! Car 816 would continue to work normally throughout the rest of this Saturday, but the following morning would be parked on the Bristol Road reservation as a prelude to its imminent scrapping at Witton depot a few weeks later. *A. K. Terry*

Above Beyond the southern bifurcation of Hazelwell Street and Pershore Road was a quarter-mile length of narrow street forming the 1890s shopping development of Stirchley. The greengrocer in his white coat and apron puts out more produce as city-bound car 830 approaches the stop beneath the Church of the Ascension; this impressive brick and stone building with its castellated tower was built in the early years of the 20th century, but gutted by fire on Thursday 28 October 1965. It stood opposite the British Oak public house, which was the site of the second Pershore Road tram short-working, numbered 46; this was a useful turn-back point for city-bound trams and the reverse crossover line can be seen in the foreground. It is Saturday 7 June 1952 and car 830 is by now looking a little less presentable than when it was used for a tour of the system by the LRTL in July 1949. Within two months the tram would be broken up at Witton depot. *J. H. Meredith*

Below Photographs like this similar, but much earlier, view of Stirchley are always difficult to date, but the style of the women's dresses and hats, the knickerbockered boys standing on the corner of Mary Vale Road and the fact that the general appearance of the clothing suggests an Edwardian summer, dates this view from about the year of the opening of the line in 1904 to about 1906. Stirchley only really grew after the opening of the Birmingham & Western Suburban railway line on 3 April 1876, and then

as an overspill area from the nearby Cadbury-owned garden suburb of Bournville. Cadbury Brothers opened the first part of their famous chocolate factory in September 1879, and in the nearby hamlet of Stirchley Street a lot of quite desirable, but less well-planned, speculative Victorian development took place. On Pershore Road the main shopping area was developed in the 1890s, so that by the time the CBT opened its line to Cotteridge the buildings were still comparatively new. The approaching CBT car, which appears to be either 163 or 168, is travelling towards Cotteridge on the single-line track passing through the by now busy shopping suburb *Author's collection*

Top Stirchley Post Office, on the left, was part of a row of converted houses dating from the 1870s. It stands just before Mayfield Road, which sounds impressive but was barely 30 yards long. The gap beyond the nearer block of buildings is occupied by Stirchley Methodist Chapel, behind its iron-railings and well-tended garden. This chapel was built in 1897, during the time when rapid urban development along Pershore Road was being funnelled along the High Street by the Birmingham & West Suburban Railway line to the west and the wet flood plain of the River Rea valley to the east. It was around the end of the 19th century that the old name of Stirchley Street was dropped. The original 'Stirchley and Breedon Cross' tram terminus was opened on 20 May 1904 just short of Fordhouse Lane, about 200 yards away beyond the distant open-top CBT-built tramcar 211, standing at the city end of the last loop before the terminus during the two-month period before the route was extended to Cotteridge. This tram was another of the CBT 'Aston'-type trams mounted on Brush-built Lycett & Conaty Radial 8ft 6in-wheelbase trucks. *Commercial postcard via Linda Chew*

Middle Car 242, later to become Birmingham Corporation 472, stands opposite Elmtree Road at the entrance to the last passing loop on the newly extended line to Cotteridge, opened on 23 June 1904. Just visible on the destination box is the paper sticker that shows the route to be 'STIRCHLEY & BREEDON CROSS', so the photograph must have been taken between the opening of that temporary terminus on 20 May 1904 and opening of the extension. To the right is the chapel on the corner of Mayfield Road. *Commercial postcard*

Bottom On a wet and miserable 27 December 1951, car 837 loads its damp passengers en route for Cotteridge at the far end of Stirchley near the Fordhouse Lane junction.

Behind the approaching Morris Ten car is the rise over the Worcester & Birmingham Canal and the former Midland Railway freight loop line. The advertisements on the hoardings are for products such as Lucas car batteries, the long-forgotten Nosegay cigarettes and St Martin's Chunky Marmalade, whose product was displayed prominently on a large number of Birmingham trams after 1951. What is amusing, with today's more health-conscious lifestyle, is the juxtaposition of the advertisements for Bass Red Triangle beer and Aspro headache-relieving tablets! Car 837 was the only member of the 812-841 Class to be repainted in the wartime all-over grey livery in January 1942, being returned to the standard simplified post-war livery in October 1946. *R. J. S. Wiseman*

Above Looking down the hill in the opposite direction from the previous view, car 836 has just left the compulsory stop beside the advertisement hoardings and is passing the newsagent's shop at the corner of Fordhouse Lane, where car 821 turned over during the Second World War (see below). This view from Breedon bridge at Lifford shows the nature of Pershore Road looking in the Stirchley Street direction, where the narrow Victorian shopping area disappears towards the one-way street system at Hazelwell Street about half a mile away. Even in the relatively traffic-free early 1950s, there are large numbers of parked vehicles, and the growth in private car ownership over the next few years would increase congestion dramatically in the late-19th-century suburbs. The tramcar, already regarded as a slow, tall, gaunt and space-consuming vehicle, was seen as an anachronism that added to the congestion, especially as kerb-side loading was rarely used in Birmingham. Until parking restrictions became the norm, trams would be impeded by stationary and manoeuvring vehicles encroaching on to the tram tracks. The anti-tram lobby used this as an argument, but interestingly the same criticism could be made of the buses of today, as parked vehicles often prevent them from reaching the kerb. *F. N. Lloyd Jones*

Below Brush-built EMB air-brake car 732 comes slowly down Breedon bridge on 15 June 1952, having stopped at the compulsory stop at the top opposite the Breedon Cross public house, in the background behind the tram. It was here that Maley & Taunton air-brake car 821 overturned on 26 October 1942. It was left unattended at the Cotteridge terminus without the handbrake being properly applied; the air brake leaked off and the tram just rolled away from the terminus, finally coming to grief at the bottom of the bridge at Fordhouse Lane, when its top deck was ripped off after it left the rails and turned over. Like many of its Class, car 732 led a fairly nomadic career following its construction in September 1926, having been at Rosebery Street, Washwood Heath and Selly Oak depots before spending its second spell at Cotteridge in the last two months of operation in 1952. *J. H. Price*

Above Opposite the Breedon Cross pub, to the right of the tram here, was the Savoy cinema, which closed on 2 February 1958 with the showing of the film *Women's Prison*. Car 838 has crested Breedon bridge and will follow the Midland Red D5B up the Victorian terrace-lined hill towards Cotteridge terminus. It is Monday 30 June 1952 and the car already carries in its balcony windows the dreaded notices warning passengers that the route will shortly be abandoned and replaced by buses. The late-Victorian/Edwardian growth of housing around the Breedon Cross was associated with the local industry that grew up around the nearby Worcester & Birmingham Canal and the former Midland Railway's lines. Industrial sites such as the Kings Norton Metal Company, which made coinage strip and blanks in copper bronze, were attracted by the advantages of cheap transport. In later years Lifford Lane led to the Kings Norton factory centre, although access was limited by the low height of a railway bridge over that road. *F. N. Lloyd Jones*

Below Once Breedon bridge was crossed, Pershore Road continued to rise steeply until it reached the ridge from which Cotteridge took its name. Immediately beyond the flatter section of the route, at Francis Road, the road crossed two railway lines, the first being the Lifford Curve linking the former Midland Railway route via Moseley and Camp Hill into Birmingham with the later 1876 Birmingham & Western Suburban line. The latter left Kings Norton station and followed the line of the Birmingham & Worcester Canal via Bournville and Selly Oak to Edgbaston before plunging through tunnels into New Street Station in the city centre. Car 823 is crossing this second bridge between Holly Road, which the Leyland Comet lorry has just passed, and Midland Road, which lies out of the picture to the left of the only city-bound motorcar in the photograph. The tram has just passed the Grant Arms tram stop at Ivy Road, the last one before the terminus. The bus stop in the foreground, for the replacement 45 bus route, is already in use for the Outer Circle service that used Pershore Road between Fordhouse Land and Cotteridge. This is the last day of tram operation along Pershore Road, and the following day a succession of Daimler CVG6s and Guy Arab IVs will operate the route. *A. K. Terry*

Above The last member of the 812 Class of Maley & Taunton air-brake bogie cars leaves Cotteridge on 6 November 1951 and passes the shops just before the junction with Midland Road. One of these shops, Wallace & Co, is a Bush dealer, and is using the expression 'wireless' rather than the later word 'radio', yet is selling the latest televisions, which, in 1951, were only just becoming available on the mass market. Shops like this would have taken advantage of the fact that the BBC had opened its Sutton Coldfield transmitter two years earlier on Saturday 17 December 1949, making television reception available in the West Midlands area. The tram will continue down the slight descent from the Cotteridge terminus over the railway bridge, the wall of which is surmounted by the distant advertising hoardings. It will then pass the Grant Arms, whose large wooden sign can just be discerned against the gable end of the furthest row of late-19th-century shops. *R. F. Mack*

Below Although seen earlier in Pebble Mill Road, this excellent close-up view of car 843 affords the opportunity to look at the salient design features of this, Birmingham's last tram, in more detail. The lightweight Brush-built car entered service in September 1930, but in the space of two years the Bolton Road and Hagley Road abandonments had taken place and the era of up-to-date AEC Regent 661 buses with a variety of 'piano-front' bodies had arrived. Their large-scale introduction effectively brought to a halt any further thoughts of tramway development in the city. Car 843 was one of the first tramcars built in this country to belong to the interesting transitional designs that developed into the more streamlined double-deckers of the mid- to late-1930s. The roughly contemporary Liverpool Cabin bogie cars, LUT No 1 and the Leeds 'Horsfield' trams, had a less traditional appearance than their predecessors, but perhaps were not as modern in their design as Blackpool Corporation's 'Balloons', Belfast's 'McCreary' cars, Edinburgh's post-1933 four-wheelers, Glasgow's 'Coronation' cars and Liverpool's 'Green Goddesses'. Birmingham's last tram still looked vaguely like the earlier Birmingham bogie cars and retained the normal standard fixtures and fittings, even a waistrail. It did, however, have a domed roof, and even if the plethora of upper-saloon side windows gave a fussy appearance, the lower saloon windows, ventilation system and destination boxes built into the side panels gave the impression of a fairly radical move towards modernity.

The tram was built because of the mutual interest of the Brush Electrical Company and Birmingham's management team in the development of lightweight tramcar construction. It is therefore not altogether surprising that the end result vaguely resembled a standard Birmingham tramcar, and a much smaller version of the cars that Brush had built for the Swansea & Mumbles system in 1928. It was fitted with two GEC WT28AS 40hp motors and weighed only 12t 6cwt 1qtr, which was 4t 9cwt less than a standard Birmingham tram. Always allocated to Cotteridge depot, it is seen in company with car 837 at Cotteridge in 1947. *A. D. Packer*

Cotteridge terminus

Below right The Edwardian shopping centre at Cotteridge was reached by CBT electric trams on 23 June 1904, Kings Norton & Northfield UDC having obtained the powers to construct the line in 1901. The large imposing tower of the then recently completed St Agnes's Church (demolished in 1986) is visible above the 11 gable-ended shops as CBT car 242 waits at the terminal stub just beyond the depot entrance line, which ran alongside the newly constructed shops to the right of the tram. This photograph was almost certainly taken in the summer of 1904, as another commercial postcard of the same tram at the temporary Stirchley terminus in May 1904 seems to feature some of the same small boys. Car 242 was one of the 239-242 Class built to a Brush design at Kyotts Lake Road Works in 1904, being among the first of CBT's 'Aston' type. They were small, being only 27ft 6in long, mounted on Brush AA 6ft 6in trucks with two 25hp Brush 1002D motors and a seating capacity of 48. Tram 242 was taken into BCT stock in January 1912 in CBT's green livery as car 472 after having been transferred from Bournbrook depot to Witton by 1907 and subsequently re-equipped with a Brush 8-foot-wheelbase truck. In 1924 it was top-covered, vestibuled and re-equipped with Dick, Kerr 6A 35hp motors. This extended its working life until June 1938, when it was withdrawn and broken up at West Smethwick depot in August. *Commercial postcard*

Below Some 47 years later, car 833 leaves the Cotteridge shopping area on 5 April 1951, while the first member of the class, 812, waits to move up to the terminus. This remained the terminus of the Pershore Road route throughout its life; although extensions were tentatively proposed towards Kings Norton, nothing came of them and further extensions to Kings Norton and West Heath were subsequently undertaken by buses. In the foreground the cloth-capped man walks across the depot line as a motor cyclist, without a crash helmet, passes the entrance. The A441 Pershore Road was the main arterial route between Birmingham and Redditch, and the Cotteridge suburban shopping centre was the last commercial area within the city boundary along this route, where the parked cars and delivery vehicles usually added to the congestion. As well as the Ford Anglia saloon, there is an Austin A40 10cwt van, a Morris-Commercial Equiload delivery van and, beyond the roller-shuttered light commercial on the nearside kerb, a Standard Vanguard van, travelling towards the city. *H. B. Priestley*

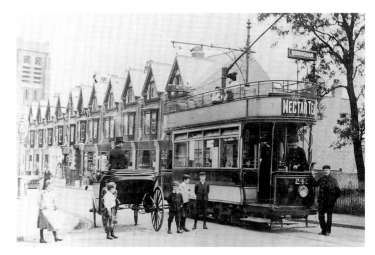

Top Experimental lightweight car 842 stands on the terminal stub of the 36 route in 1952, in company with car 822. St Agnes's Church and the row of shops still remain from the previous view, but the open space beyond the depot entrance has been filled by the stone-faced Barclays Bank, standing behind the utility bus shelters for the Outer Circle bus route. Originally there were two curves into the depot so that trams could turn towards the city or to the single parking line, which extended about 30 yards to a position opposite Watford Road. By 1952 only the southern curve remained, which meant that all cars leaving or returning to the depot had to be re-poled after a reversing operation. Car 842 is one of the two lightweight cars allocated to Cotteridge depot, but as we have seen it is doubtful whether either was going to become the precursor of a new fleet. However, they did signal the way the Transport Department was thinking in terms of a modern tram design. By the time this photograph was taken, the splendid-looking all-metal Short Brothers tram had been mounted on the Maley & Taunton bogies from the runaway tram, 821, which altered it from the lowest to the highest bogie car in the fleet after 1950, giving it a rather perched look. *Author's collection*

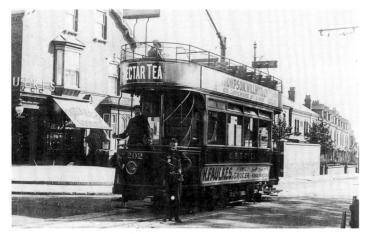

Middle The Cotteridge area of Kings Norton UDC was still relatively new when CBT car 202, painted in the Munich Lake and Cream livery, was photographed at the terminus in about 1905. This 48-seat open-topped tram was built by Brush in 1904 and operated for much of its CBT life from Witton. It was thought that, after being allocated to Bournbrook depot for its first four months of service, which included Cotteridge as an outlying sub-depot, car 202 was transferred to Witton, the northern operational base for the CBT, opened on 1 October 1904, yet here it is in Cotteridge carrying two advertisements for shops on the south side of Birmingham. That on the rocker panel is for H. Faulkes, Family Grocer, whose premises are behind the tram on the corner of Watford Road. After being transferred to the Corporation fleet on 1 January 1912, CBT 202 became car 462. This 'Aston'-type car was eventually top-covered in 1924 and was finally withdrawn in May 1938. *Lens of Sutton*

Bottom Almost 40 years later little has changed at Cotteridge, although the walls in front of the houses beyond the tram in Pershore Road were removed to accommodate retail premises at about the time of the First World War. Outside the entrance tracks to Cotteridge depot we take another look at one of Birmingham's two last trams, the lightweight 842. Although neither was officially regarded as a precursor to the next generation of trams, it is interesting to speculate what might have been had not the Coventry Road routes been converted to trolleybuses and had the diesel-engined Daimler COG5 not been the revolutionary success it obviously became! The tram driver has stopped beneath the blackout trough on the overhead, which enabled the conductor, who is in the middle of swinging around the trolleypole, to do so without the inevitable sparks being visible to enemy aircraft. Car 842 is still mounted on its original English Electric Burnley-style maximum-traction bogies with their 26-inch-diameter driving wheels, making the tramcar, with its two 40hp DK T105/3KP motors, the lowest in the fleet at 15ft 6in. It retained the pre-war livery until June 1947, although because of its modern style the livery change only involved the omission of the gold lining-out and the vertical blue lining on the corners between the decks. Car 842 was destined to be the last to travel into the city from Cotteridge depot on Sunday 6 July 1952, and was in such good condition that it was briefly made available for sale in working order for £25! Interest was shown by a North Wales operator, but by this time it had been dismantled and sent to W. T. Bird's yard, where it survived, in two halves, for more than a year. *Burrows Brothers*

Top right On a sunny spring morning in 1951 car 836 waits in the single line opposite the entrance to Cotteridge depot before the driver clocks in at the Bundy clock and starts off on the 5-mile run to the city terminus at Navigation Street. These Maley & Taunton-bogied, Short Brothers-bodied cars of 1928 were regarded by the motormen as the best of all the 63hp air-brake trams; although not usually able to produce sparkling performances on the Pershore Road route, they were reliable and comfortable vehicles. Beyond, one of the earlier Brush-built EMB cars, 758, waits to move up to the terminus stop once the eight-windowed 836 starts its city-bound journey. It has just been passed by a Midland Red SOS FEDD (Front Entrance Double-Decker) working on the 147 route from Redditch. It is still painted in the pre-spray-painted style of livery; this was replaced by an all-over red colour scheme, causing the silver roof and lining to be lost. *G. W. Morant*

Above The entrance to Cotteridge depot was sandwiched between ladies' and gentlemen's public lavatories, the former visible behind the 1936 Morris Eight to the right of the telephone box; the Bundy clock used for registering departure times from the terminus can also be seen. The trams passed through the narrow depot entrance into the yard on a single line. When it was first opened by CBT in June 1904, it was little more than a sub-depot to Bournbrook, with a capacity for only eight trams. It was subsequently taken over by BCT and extended in 1920-21 at a cost of £16,439 to its maximum capacity of 33 tramcars. It closed to bus operation on 25 October 1986. Brush-built car 811, the last of the 40 EMB air-brake cars of 1928, has just moved off the single-line stub for its return trip to Birmingham. It was transferred from Selly Oak on 15 May 1952 and would see out the last six weeks of its service life from Cotteridge. *R. Brook*

Above Looking quite smart, if a little dusty, car 831 waits in the toilet-flanked single-track depot entrance on 27 June 1952. This 62-seat tramcar, despite its traditional looks, was as advanced as anything contemporarily being introduced elsewhere in the country. It had two English Electric DK 30/L 63hp motors, Maley & Taunton air-brakes, Maley & Taunton-built Burnley-style maximum-traction bogies, and Short Brothers bodies with an eight-windowed top-deck, built on underframes supplied by Brush. Eight days later, the day before the Cotteridge route closure, 831 was moved to Kyotts Lake Road, then in August it was driven across the city to Witton, where 56

of the Bristol Road-Cotteridge vehicles were broken up. *G. F. Douglas*

Below Brush lightweight tramcar 843 did not fare as well as its slightly heavier twin because it was pared down to the absolute minimum; at an unladen weight of 12t 6cwt 2qtr, it was 1⅓ tons lighter than 842, and almost 4½ tons lighter than the standard air-brake tramcars of 1926-28. In 1946 it is seen in Cotteridge depot yard looking distinctly careworn and slightly shabby. The yard opened out into a fan of eight tracks, and 843 is standing on the one nearest the depot's offices. Car 843 lost its pre-war livery in March 1948 and during the following July was back in the works for further remedial action to the lightweight floors. The lightweight body structure was about at the end of its life, with buckled lower body panels and a defective motor, when the tram was withdrawn early from service in January 1952. It had covered 432,500 miles, 50,000 less than its sister 842, and 180,000 less than the maximum achieved by any of Cotteridge depot's 812 Class. *M. J. O'Connor*

Opposite above Although somewhat cramped, Cotteridge depot's eight tracks were generally sufficient to cope with the needs of the 36 route cars. On the occasion of an enthusiasts' tour on 17 June 1951, cars 836, 842 and 837 stand in the depot, the lightweight car 842 having

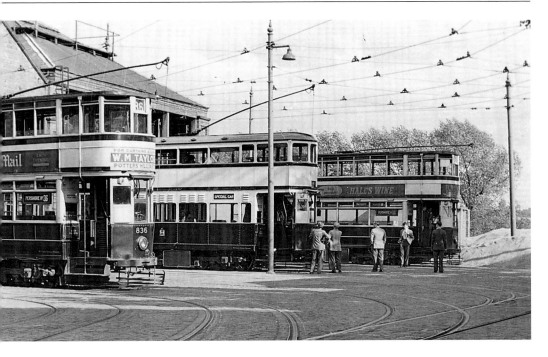

been used as the tour vehicle. It sits higher on the track, and the shape of the valance between the bogies is much more rectangular, following its rebuild with the bogies from car 821. Although it is perhaps difficult to see the difference in height between the standard Birmingham tramcar and the experimental tram, 842 was only 15ft 3in to the top of the trolleybase, although its more modern body shape gives the impression of being even lower. *Author's collection*

Right For the tram enthusiast, the sight of a depot in the throes of being prepared for its conversion to bus operation was always a depressing one. This process was usually undertaken in the months prior to the change-over, and consisted of the tram pits being filled in and new bus maintenance pits being constructed. During the spring of 1952 the bulldozer and cement-mixers moved into Cotteridge depot, as they had done at nearby Selly Oak depot some months earlier, and began the work that was the prelude to the abandonment. The trams, soon to be made redundant, were regarded as time-expired, expendable commodities; repairs were reduced to a minimum to save unnecessary expense, which resulted in three of Cotteridge's tramcars being withdrawn early as a result of problems that would previously have been regarded as fairly trivial. Looking for all the world like condemned prisoners, cars

748, the ubiquitous 842 and 816 stand between the conversion work and the entrance. Although they have a few months of work in front of them, the end of their service careers is in sight with the steady, slow run-down of this penultimate south-western part of the Birmingham tram system. *Author's collection*

MOSELEY ROAD ROUTES

The Moseley Road and Alcester Road services were a complicated inheritance for Birmingham Corporation from the City of Birmingham Tramways Company on the expiry of the former's steam tram leases on 31 December 1906. There were two basic groups of routes, those starting in the Hill Street/Navigation Street area, which corresponded with the former CBT steam services, and the later routes that began from the High Street area. Each of these groups of routes had various short-workings and those from the Hill Street termini are shown in the accompanying maps.

Hill Street/Navigation Street services

The original steam tram service to Moseley was opened by Birmingham Central Tramways on 28 December 1884, from Moat Row via Bradford Street and Moseley Road. This was extended on 20 June 1885 via Bromsgrove Street, Station Street and the newly opened John Bright Street to the terminus in Hill Street. It later served as the basis of the High Street routes.

The second route to open was that through Balsall Heath, which began operation on 19 July 1886 to join the main Moseley Road route about half a mile north of the terminus at St Mary's Row. The final mile to the Kings Heath terminus near Kings Heath depot at Silver Street was opened on 1 February 1887.

On the expiry of the CBT lease on 31 December 1906 the system was transferred to the Corporation, which began operation with electric top-covered Radial cars of the 71 Class. There were three main routes that began around the corner site near New Street Station's Queens Drive:

- the long Alcester Lanes End route via Balsall Heath, later to be numbered 39, which started in Hill Street
- the Cannon Hill branch service to Willows Road, Edgbaston, which in the 1915 route numbering system became the 37; originally it had its terminus in Navigation Street at the Queens Hotel end, but in May 1944 exchanged its starting point with
- the Leopold Street and Highgate 41 route, which went from Hill Street.

The three routes left the side of New Street Station and travelled past Station Street, which was the terminus for the Coventry Road and Stratford Road tram services. After crossing Smallbrook Street the trams passed the Empire and Hippodrome theatres and continued along Hurst Street, with its rather run-down Victorian shops and nearby market warehouses. The tracks into Bromsgrove Street were retained after the closure of the Stratford Road group of tram routes in January 1937, to enable Selly Oak, Cotteridge and Rosebery Street cars to reach Kyotts Lake Road Works. At the Sherlock Street junction the routes diverged.

Leopold Street

Crossing Sherlock Street, the outward-bound trams on the Leopold Street routes continued along a short section of Hurst Street before turning right into Bishop Street and, less than 100 yards later, turning left into MacDonald Street where they met the inbound track. Trams from Leopold Street going to the city continued to the MacDonald Street-Sherlock Street junction before turning right and then left into Hurst Street. The accompanying map shows the details.

This was an area of back-to-back and three-storey housing of the worst sort; decaying unsanitary houses were mixed with industrial premises, yet out of this unpromising mixture came a sense of community that subsequent urban renewal schemes failed to reproduce.

From MacDonald Street the tram route turned into Thomas Street, then into Leopold Street. The appalling inner city Victorian houses here were demolished in one of Birmingham's few pre-war housing redevelopment schemes at St Martin's Flats, completed in 1939. Between the wars Birmingham built an unprecedented 50,000 new houses, but these were mainly on the large outer municipal housing estates, many of which would never see a tram service.

Once past the flats the trams climbed the steep 1 in 13 hill in Leopold Street, passing the usual mixture of old housing and factories, before cresting the hill and taking the tight curve into Moseley Road. Here the trams ran among the Moseley Road cars, usually only as far as Trafalgar Road and the adjacent tram depot, although a few peak-hour runs did go to Moseley, Kings Heath and Alcester Lanes End.

The steep gradient of Leopold Street meant that extra care had to be taken, especially when descending the hill. The 401 Class, delivered from UEC in 1912-13 and fitted with Mountain & Gibson 7ft 6in trucks, were after several months fitted with the Spencer-Dawson air and oil brake, which failed in the 'on' position. These 50 trams ran for the rest of their working lives on the routes operated by Moseley Road depot, although the newer 702 Class operated on Sundays on the Leopold Street route until 1939.

Balsall Heath and Cannon Hill

The outward route of the 37 and 39 Balsall Heath and Cannon Hill trams turned right from Hurst Street into Sherlock Street. Leaving behind the inbound line at Gooch Street, the route turned left into St Lukes Road and into an area of early-Victorian detached housing, which had seen far better days.

St Lukes Road made a long right turn to cross Belgrave Road and the Inner Circle No 8 bus route. The trams then continued along Alexandra Road, with its late-19th-century terraced, bay-windowed houses, before turning left into Balsall Heath Road. The cars stopped outside the Balsall Heath Picture House, which was the start of Balsall Heath's shopping area; they then immediately turned to the right into Clevedon Road and away from the shops.

City-bound trams crossed Balsall Heath Road a little further beyond the turn, so cars travelling in the opposite direction could, at this point, be seen scurrying from Cox Street West into the shop-lined Longmore Street. This part of the Balsall Heath system was characterised by the movement of trams following meandering courses, turning this way and that, in a maze of narrow streets. As a result, this section of the route was known locally by staff and enthusiasts alike as 'the Chinese Railway', although it would appear that the logic for this has to rank with other local expressions such as 'Going round Bill's mother's' when describing a circuitous journey!

Meanwhile, outbound trams continued south-westwards along Clevedon Road, at the back of Calthorpe Park, then swung round a left and right curve before entering Court Road, which was the last section of the route common to both services.

Cannon Hill

On reaching Edward Road the 37 and 39 tram routes diverged at the Cannon Hill public house on a triangular track layout. The 37 to Cannon Hill crossed Edward Road and turned into the more affluent residential Cannon Hill Road. This was the start of a mile-long anti-clockwise loop via Edgbaston Road (where it passed the entrance to Cannon Hill Park), Willows Road (where the terminus was situated), and Hallam Street. From the latter, the 37 route went back to Edward Road, but this time at its junction with Lincoln Street. Going round similar large, one-way loops on other tram systems was sometimes known as 'Cannon Hilling', a term coined by Wingate H. Bett, the well-known ticket authority.

City-bound 37 route cars went straight across Edward Road into Lincoln Street, then at Balfour Street they were joined again by the inbound 39 Balsall Heath services coming from Moseley and Kings Heath.

Balsall Heath

At Court Road, the 39 route trams going to Moseley, Kings Heath and Alcester Lanes End parted from the 37 route and turned left, eastwards, into Edward Road and proceeded along a mixed Victorian residential and retail area. This was again single-line working, but trams regularly travelled in the opposite direction from Moseley Road, enabling them to get to either the Cannon Hill triangle from Moseley Road depot, or to undertake other depot workings to Lincoln Street, for the inbound Cannon Hill route. Depot workings used the tracks at the eastern, Moseley Road, end, which had been used for the circular Leopold Street-Balsall Heath service that lasted for only one week after its introduction on 1 January 1907.

The Balsall Heath trams travelled as far as Mary Street on their way out of the city before turning right and beginning the climb past the last of the Victorian terraces to the 49 route's short-working cross-over at Edgbaston Road. Beyond here the tram route continued into Park Road and passed through an area of better-quality houses and villas, built as a continuation of the expansion of Moseley when the railway was attracting Victorian commuters.

The Balsall Heath tramcars emerged from Park Road into Alcester Road to join the trams that had started from High Street and had taken the more direct route along Moseley Road. Those going to Alcester Lanes End carried on along Alcester Road to nearby Moseley and Kings Heath.

On their return to the city, having descended Park Road and Mary Street, the inbound 39 route cars crossed Edward Road and turned left from Mary Street into a short length of Balfour Street. They then turned right into Lincoln Street where they joined the inbound Cannon Hill service and carried on through Cox Street West and into the start of the shopping area in Longmore Street.

The inner area of the city contained great swathes of sub-standard property and it was through an increasingly deteriorating landscape that the trams ran for some 42 years noisily, slowly, but unerringly. The houses in the Balfour Street and Cox Street West area were not the worst in the city, but not many years after the trams had finally been withdrawn this area was totally cleared, so that today the area to the north of Balsall Heath Road is virtually unidentifiable.

After crossing Belgrave Road, the trams returning to the city entered the busy Gooch Street, which after turning sharply to the north-west at Highgate Street, carried on for some 600 yards before regaining Sherlock Street. Here the trams turned right, crossing the outbound line of the Balsall Heath trams

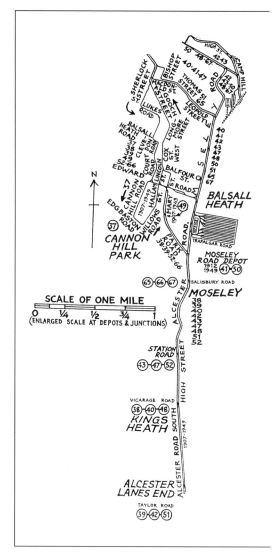

and almost immediately being joined, from MacDonald Street, by the city-bound trams returning from Leopold Street. At this point all the routes turned left into Hurst Street and climbed towards the city termini in Hill Street or Navigation Street.

High Street services

The High Street services were introduced on 6 September 1909 in an attempt to get passengers to the other side of the city centre. Inbound, the cars, which had climbed the Bull Ring's steep hill, passed the spiritual heart of Birmingham,

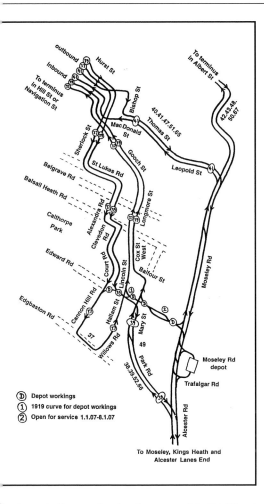

A schematic diagram showing the routes of the 37, 39 and 41 tram services round 'the Chinese Railway', together with depot workings from Moseley Road depot. For clarity each outbound and inbound journey is shown as a separate line – the system map (left) shows which tracks were single and which double.

the parish church of St Martin, before turning right alongside Oswald Bailey's Army & Navy stores and into Moor Street. Here the road again climbed, although this time not so steeply, as it left the bustling markets of the Bull Ring and passed the Great Western Railway's little Edwardian gem of Moor Street Station and, beyond that, the imposing Moor Street Warehouse. Once over the GWR railway bridge, the trams turned left into Carrs Lane, passing the mock-Tudor Corner public house on the left and the austere, classically inspired Congregational church of 1820.

The original terminus was in the short length of High Street between the top of Carrs Lane and the next turn to the right, Albert Street. This arrangement lasted until 1921 when a new central loading island in Dale End was used as the terminus, together with trams going to Coventry and Stratford Roads. Although the structure was impressive, its complicated tramcar access made it something of an operating millstone; thus in 1930 the Moseley Road trams were transferred to Albert Street outside the Beehive department store.

After leaving the distinctive canopied shelters at the top of Albert Street, the 'main line' Moseley Road route to Alcester Lanes End, numbered 42, descended to the junction with Moor Street and turned right, passing some elegant early-Georgian houses, including, on the corner of New Meeting Street, the former Dingley's Hotel, which had a particularly fine baroque frontage. At the bottom of Carrs Lane the outward-going trams completed their loop and met the inbound cars.

Having turned left into the Bull Ring, the Moseley Road trams followed the same route as the Coventry Road, Stratford Road and Warwick Road, and Stechford tram services; they descended past Digbeth Police Station at the corner of Meriden Street and proceeded along the busy shopping and warehouse area that was to be found in Digbeth. Digbeth was part of the Anglo-Saxon settlement of Birmingham and it was shortly before the original fording point of the River Rea that the Moseley-bound trams left the main thoroughfare and turned right into Rea Street, later to become better known as the home of the Midland Red's Digbeth bus garage and coach station.

A short length of the industrially lined Rea Street was traversed before the route turned left into the wide Bradford Street, which led from the markets area towards Camp Hill. The tram route then climbed through an area of heavy industry before turning right into Moseley Road. This section, from Rea Street, followed the route of the 1884 steam trams.

Once into Moseley Road, the tram route passed Highgate Park and the splendid Elizabethan Stratford House before meeting the Leopold Street trams some 200 yards further on. Passing through Balsall Heath's late-Victorian civic buildings, the straight run along Moseley Road led to the tram depot at Trafalgar Road, opened for the Corporation takeover on 1 January 1907. Trafalgar Road was also the terminus of the usual Leopold Street services.

The nature of the route changed beyond the depot from an artisans' industrial area to the late-19th-century tree-lined residential suburb of Moseley. On the climb from the tram depot, the Balsall Heath route joined the main route at Park Road, and from here for the remaining 2 miles of the route to Alcester Lanes End, the 39 and 42 routes ran together. Moseley Village, at the junction with St Mary's Row, was reached next, with its high-quality shopping and air of prosperity. This was the turn-back point for the 65, 66 and 67 short-workings.

Beyond Moseley, the trams went uphill, passing Moseley Hall and Reddings Road, home of Moseley Rugby Football Club, before descending Welsh's Hill to the bridge over the former Midland Railway line just east of Kings Heath station at Queensbridge Road.

The major shopping centre of Kings Heath was reached next; this had been a small village until the mid-19th century, but the extension of the CBT steam tram service on 1 February 1887 had the usual effect of encouraging urban growth. The former steam tram depot, coke yard and pits at Silver Street were passed on the right; this had been opened in 1887 and had a capacity of about 20 trams. After the closure of the steam tram system on New Year's Eve 1906 the depot was brought back into use by the Corporation on 1 April 1908; it continued to be used until 31 December 1911, when it was finally closed, although the building survives to this day. Further along the shop-lined High Street, beyond the steam tram terminus, was the Victorian All Saints Church at the corner of Vicarage Road where, in later years, the Outer Circle, 11, bus route crossed Alcester Road South. It was also the turn-back point for the 38, 40 and 48 routes.

Beyond here the Alcester Road South section of the route began, descending gently to Howard Road before climbing the remaining half-mile to the terminus. This was just beyond Taylor Road at Alcester Lanes End, opposite the Kings Arms public house, a hostelry always known locally as 'the Knob'. The terminus here was always busy, especially so when there was a meeting at Kings Heath dog track.

After the war the 42 route was usually worked by the open-balconied 401 Class, so there was frequently a mix of these and the 702 Class bogie cars working the 39 service to Balsall Heath at the terminus.

Balsall Heath: Navigation Street to Bromsgrove Street

Car 702, the first of the Brush-built bogie cars of 1926, stands in Navigation Street waiting to leave on the 37 route to Cannon Hill. Just over the shoulder of the woman with the child can be seen the lower saloon door of the tram with the 'key' symbol of the Birmingham Municipal Bank etched on the glass. The Futurist Cinema is showing the film *White Woman* starring the English-born character actor Charles Laughton and Carole Lombard. She later married Clark Gable and was tragically killed in January 1942 when the aircraft in which she was travelling crashed in a blizzard in the USA. It is Monday 30 April 1934, the day that the British Government set up a feasibility study investigating a public television service, which, in the fullness of time, would sound the death knell for the majority of Birmingham's cinemas. *J. E. Cull*

Right A positively gleaming car 415 stands at the Queens Hotel end of Navigation Street, working on the 41 route via Leopold Street; it will turn back outside the Moseley Road tram depot at Trafalgar Road. The car is ex-works, having been repainted on 5 April 1938; its condition suggests that the photograph was taken shortly afterwards. It is carrying an enamel advertisement for Whitbread's Ale & Stout, a common, conservative addition to numerous tramcars in the 1930s. This spring morning scene also has in the background a Guinness advertisement depicting the Spreading Chestnut Tree, which was displayed in 1938. Behind the tramcar is the roof of New Street Station which, when constructed, was the largest canopy roof in the world, with a span of 212 feet. It was badly damaged during an air raid on 26 October 1940 and was dismantled over a 15-month period to February 1947 by the aptly named Altitude Contracting Co Ltd of Birmingham. *R. T. Wilson*

Below In the late summer of 1949, car 328 stands against the kerb in Navigation Street next Finlay's tobacconist kiosk. Passengers board this Moseley Road extra on the 70 route to Rednal while the driver and an inspector struggle with the points that will enable car 328 to use the cross-over to gain John Bright Street. Meanwhile, car 435

unloads directly into Navigation Street after arriving from Moseley Road on the 41 route. Towering over the scene is the Queens Hotel, opened on 1 June 1854, rebuilt during 1911 and extended in 1925 by adding an extra two storeys. With the war came a slow loss of its importance; after suffering a general deterioration of the fabric of the station through lack of maintenance, by the time the last Moseley Road trams were running the hotel's 'glory days' had gone. It was proposed to build a new hotel and offices in 1960 when the first New Street rebuilding plans were announced, but these were altered and by 1964 the final plans were without the hotel and the old premises were finally closed in 1966. *F. N. Lloyd Jones*

Top Only two of the 401 Class tramcars were repainted in grey livery, the first being 449, in December 1942. Despite the lack of blue paint, the paintshop at Kyotts Lake Road gave the grey a coat of varnish, so although dowdy, the tram still looked smart. It is standing in Hill Street alongside the wall of New Street Station on Thursday 20 May 1943 when working on the 39 route to Alcester Lanes End via Balsall Heath. The tram's trolleypole has been positioned beneath the blackout anti-spark trough on the overhead. The second grey tram was 421, repainted in April 1943; both were repainted into fleet livery during August 1945. *G. F. Cunningham, NTM, Crich*

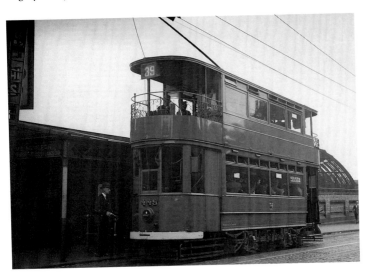

Middle The 37 route originally terminated in Navigation Street, but after 1 May 1944 it started in Hill Street near the junction with Queens Drive, whose finial-topped gates are visible behind car 728 as it stands next to the shelters on 30 September 1947. This tram had returned to Moseley Road only one month before, having been at Witton depot since April 1939. The conductor is about to put the trolleypole on to the overhead while intending passengers to Balsall Heath and Cannon Hill board the tram. The side destination blind has been wound round the wrong way on the top spindle, causing the lettering to slope backwards. *J. H. Price*

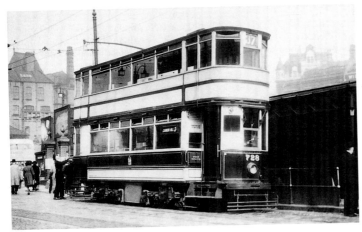

Bottom Having arrived at the terminus in Hill Street, car 448 unloads its passengers outside the bomb site that had once been the Malt Shovel public house, which received a direct hit on 19/20 November 1940. Despite not having been repainted for about seven years, this UEC-bodied 54-seat tramcar of early 1913 still looks smart in its slightly lustreless pre-war livery. The notices in the tram windows and the summer dresses of the women and girls suggests that this could have been an August Bank Holiday, and the people all seem to be making a 'bee-line' for Navigation Street where the tramcars left for the 8-mile ride 'out to the Lickeys'. The distant car 372, loading at the shelters, is working on the 37 service to Cannon Hill; this tramcar was transferred to Moseley Road depot in August 1945 and stayed until November 194<??>. Just visible on the extreme left is a pre-war Daimler COG5 Corporation bus climbing Hill Street; its rear dome is still in camouflage paint, all suggesting that this photograph was taken in 1946. *C. Carter*

Above One can almost sense the wonderful smell of sulphur as a steam locomotive passes beneath the Hill Street bridge, leaving behind a swathe of drifting smoke. Brand new Midland Red Brush-bodied AEC Regent II 3106 (JHA 7) is working into the city on the 130 route from Stourbridge in 1949. These AD2 types were the first to have the Midland Red-designed tin front, but their continued use on the main Hagley Road run from Birmingham ended within a few years as, despite their modern looks, they only had an AEC 7.58-litre diesel engine, which left them very underpowered with a full load. Tramcar 717 is unloading passengers at Severn Street after working the 39 route from Alcester Lanes End. The bomb-destroyed structures on the corner of Hill Street and John Bright Street are again the remains of the Malt Shovel. *F. N. Lloyd Jones*

Below The first of the UEC-bodied Spencer-Dawson oil and air brake cars unloads its passengers at the tram and trolleybus stop outside the Empire Palace in Hill Street at the junction with Smallbrook Street. It is on the 41 route and will follow the Leyland Titan PD2/1 1701 (HOV 701) and the unusual Park Royal-bodied RT-type AEC 'Regent' III 1632 (GOE 632) up Hill Street to the terminus at Navigation Street. The Empire Palace, the tall building with the round windows, opened in May 1894 and became part of the Moss Empire group of theatres. Unlike that graveyard of English comedians, the Glasgow Empire, the Birmingham theatre failed to survive the Second World War and was gutted in an air raid in 1941, leaving only the shell intact. It was demolished in about 1951. *R. T. Wilson*

Below If traffic conditions were like they are today, one can imagine an irate motorist's reaction at being stuck behind a tram unloading passengers in the middle of the road with the traffic lights on green! Fortunately it is February 1949 and the amount of traffic is minimal. However, the passengers who have just disembarked from car 729 and are walking out from behind it to cross Hurst Street will have had to watch carefully as the large 1936 Austin saloon, probably an Eighteen, proceeds southward away from the city. It can be seen that, like many of Birmingham's roads, Hurst Street was cobbled. What is interesting is the distinct change in the pattern of the cobbles; as already mentioned, the 18 inches or so on either side of the track was the responsibility of the Tramways Department, while from there to the kerb had to be maintained by the Highways Department. The vaguely 'Arabian Nights' structure above the tram – looking like an decorative feature added to the tram by the Brush Company – is in fact the top of the tower of the Birmingham Hippodrome; still there today, it is the permanent home of the Birmingham Royal Ballet, a far cry from when the great Max Miller 'trod the boards' there! *F. N. Lloyd Jones*

Bottom The Hippodrome tower is still visible as car 721 stands in Hurst Street at the junction with Bromsgrove Street on its way to Cannon Hill on 14 April 1938. The tracks leading in from the right used to carry the trams to Coventry Road and Stratford Road, but it has been some 16 months since the most recent abandonment on the latter, and the tracks are now only used for trams going to the works. This section of Hurst Street was wired for the inbound Coventry Road trolleybuses that would terminate in Station Street. The Davenports public house is still trading today as the Australian Bar, but virtually every other building was swept away in the late 1980s to create the new Arcadian shopping precinct and its numerous Chinese supermarkets and restaurants. The entrance to the precinct is approximately where the following tram, car 428, working on the Leopold Road service, is standing. *H. B. Priestley*

Right At the bottom end of Hurst Street, away from the theatres around Smallbrook Street, was the start of the market and industrial area near the edge of the city. The large city public houses gave way to small Victorian corner 'locals', and the remnants of the worst of the mid-Victorian back-to-back houses that had escaped the bombs of the Second World War were mixed, often somewhat uncomfortably, with piecemeal inter-war industrial development. Car 442 has stopped at the bottom of Hurst Street and will take the line off to the left on the photograph, which will take it into Sherlock Street. The track to the right is the outward Leopold Street line. *F. N. Lloyd Jones*

Below right Looking down Hurst Street towards the junction, we see where the 37 route to Cannon Hill and the 39 route through Balsall Heath and Park Road to Moseley and beyond parted company; the latter turned right into Sherlock Street, while the short section of Hurst Street between the cafe and the public house in the centre of the picture took the 41 group of routes towards Leopold Street via Bishop Street and MacDonald Street. The Blue Cafe on the corner of Sherlock Street is advertising 'a variety of sandwiches' – the three alternatives of meat, cheese and lettuce sound distinctly unappetising, but in 1949 there was still rationing, resulting in such meagre fare being offered. Car 717 is about to take the right turn in front of the White Swan public house. This bogie tram, built in 1926 by Brush, was equipped with EMB bogies and GEC WT32H 40hp motors; although a trifle slow compared to other bogie cars, these 702 Class trams were well suited to the Balsall Heath routes. This tram

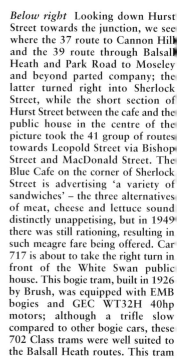

had been transferred from Witton at the end of August 1947 and it is seen towards the end of its 26-month sojourn at Moseley Road; after that depot closed 717 would go to Miller Street, where it would work until the final day's operation of tramcars in Birmingham on Saturday 4 July 1953. *R. T. Wilson*

Leopold Street

Above This closer 1949 view of the junction seen in the previous photograph shows the short length of cobbled road taken by the 41 route trams between the run-down, three-storey terraces and small workshops that were such a common feature of inner Birmingham. The White Swan seems more intent on advertising its allegiance to Ansells brewery than its name; standing on the southern corner of Hurst Street and Sherlock Street, it dates from about the end of the 1920s and sits rather uncomfortably among the older run-down property. Car 401, working on the 41

route, is passing a 1947 Bradford van and will turn right into Bishop Street then left into MacDonald Street, where it will meet the inbound cars. The latter continued along MacDonald Street to meet Sherlock Street, to the right of the photograph, turning right to join the route of the city-bound services via Gooch Street. *R. T. Wilson*

Below On its outward-bound journey, car 416 has just turned from Bishop Street to meet the inbound track of the 41 route in MacDonald Street, and has stopped just beyond the Belisha beacon at the Barford Street stop. The Belisha crossing has no 'zebra' markings on the road, these being applied in 1951, and then generally only on roads with a tarmacked surface. The extent of the damage done during the then recent wartime bombing in this area can be seen, with at least four sites being visible; a colloquial expression for these derelict areas was a 'bomb-building-site'. For children growing up in the early post-war years, these potentially dangerous places were secret dens, battlefields, football pitches and places in which to play hide and seek. Gradually, as the inner slum clearance schemes began, the old houses on either side of these sites were demolished and with them went the bomb-sites. Car 416 will proceed on its brief journey via the short length of Thomas Street towards its destination of Trafalgar Road. *R. T. Wilson*

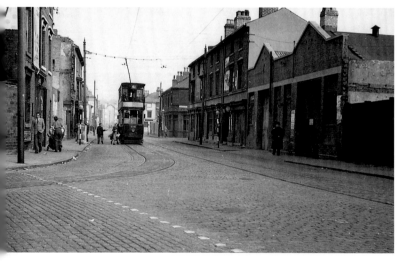

Right Open-balconied car 430 has just descended Leopold Street on its way into the city on the 41 route in 1939, having just left the stop outside the school at the corner of Dymoke Street; the junction in the foreground is at Vaughton Street. The tram will turn slightly left and travel along Thomas Street into MacDonald Street. Just visible above the hoardings is the St Martin's Estate, an experimental block of interconnected four-storey concrete flats built between 1937 and 1939; they contained 266 units and marked a huge step forward in the thinking of Birmingham Council. In the inter-war period the Council had constructed a mere 355 new

dwellings in the central wards of the city, when realistically a wholesale redevelopment should have taken place during the 1930s. The flats were, however, not a success. Water seepage into the concrete blocks resulted in their early fame being quickly replaced by notoriety. By the late 1970s the *Birmingham Evening Mail* referred to them as 'the rambling run-down warren of 266 problem flats'. In 1981 they were demolished! *Author's collection*

Below Car 426, working the 41 route, cautiously descends Leopold Street using its air and oil brake equipment to control and, where necessary, stop the tram on the 1 in 13 gradient. The fitting of this brake to the 401

Class in the latter half of 1913 raised the unladen weight of the trams by 12cwt to 13t 2cwt. The Leopold Street trams ran through an industrial landscape as the route climbed the hill towards Moseley Road. In this inner area of Highgate there was a mixture of back-to-back houses dating from the middle of the 19th century as well as later Victorian terraces. The true nature of the gradient can be assessed by the angle of the wartime Bedford OW lorry as it struggles up the hill. It is to be hoped that the parked American lorry will not obstruct the Bedford as the tram passes them both. *F. N. Lloyd Jones*

Below Four-wheeled tram 416 passes a parked 1938-registered Austin 10 on the steepest part of Leopold Street. On the right are the premises of Samuel Heath & Sons, whose brass foundry has been on this site since 1830. Throughout the inner part of Highgate, small specialised foundries and manufacturing companies grew up in the 19th century, and around them developed the workers' houses. This scene was captured by Noel Lloyd Jones on the last day of operation of the Leopold Street service; he comprehensively covered the Birmingham system on film from 1948 until 1953, and many of his excellent pictures appear in this book. Although he retired to live in Lancashire, he had a great affection for the Birmingham system, reflected in his photographs. *F. N. Lloyd Jones*

Top Car 419, on the 37 route, is seen climbing Leopold Street on 10 June 1941. Because of track damage this route was diverted via the 41 route to Moseley Road, then via the depot working line in Edward Road to regain the Cannon Hill lines. The tram's headlight is fitted with a blackout deflection mask, its fenders are painted white, and its windows have been covered by anti-blast netting, which was glued on and made the auxiliary conductors' travel even less enjoyable, as only a small square was kept clear.

Things got so bad in the blackout that volunteers travelled on the trams and buses to call out to the passengers where they had got to. A temporary blast shelter has been made at the entrance to the industrial premises on the left; this and all the street furniture has been marked in white so as to stand out at night. On this bleak wartime day in 1941, Hitler's deputy, Rudolf Hess, crash-landed his aeroplane near Glasgow and began one of the Second World War's most bizarre episodes. *W. A. Camwell*

Middle After leaving Moseley Road on the return journey into the city centre, car 426 has stopped on the brow of the steep section of Leopold Street. A compulsory red tram stop at the top of a descent was a regular safety feature on every route in the city, and here it was particularly necessary. At the top of Leopold Street the land use changed and became far more residential. The houses were not the awful back-to-backs, but the later 1880s style of terrace, although they still opened out directly on to the street. The archway on the right was built to allow horse-drawn wagons to gain access to the workshops behind. This area was typical of the city's central wards, with nearly every corner having either a pub or a shop. *F. N. Lloyd Jones*

Bottom Once at the summit of Leopold Street the trams dropped gently to reach Moseley Road, where the four-wheel cars squealed as their rigid wheelbases took the tightly radiused turn. As at a number of sharp curves, water was used as a lubricant, and the rail in Moseley Road had a small drain to allow the water to drain away. Car 402, with three schoolboys riding on the balcony, is about to take the turn in front of Perks's iron and steel scrap merchants offices. This 1949 view shows the final state of the 401 Class cars that served the Moseley Road faithfully for all but a few months of their 37-year service life. At 29ft 9in long over fenders, these 1913-built trams were only 3ft 9in shorter than the first bogie cars delivered the following year. They originally had identical electrical equipment to the 512 Class, yet were 3¼ tons lighter, so their performance on Moseley Road was comparatively lively. The 41 route continued along Moseley Road only as far as Trafalgar Road. This route via Leopold Street was the shortest, and was the normal service after 1939 as the 40 route to Kings

Heath only ran at peak periods, while the 51 route to Alcester Lanes End only had occasional journeys. Before the Second World War there was also a Sunday 51 service operated by 702 Class bogie cars. *R. T. Wilson*

Sherlock Street to Cannon Hill

Below right A large Austin Eighteen taxi speeds past the Sherlock Street junction with Gooch Street (on the left) and overtakes car 729 on its way to Cannon Hill. Gooch Street was used for the inbound 37 and 39 routes, while the outward routes continued along Sherlock Street before turning left at St Lukes Road, the third junction after Gooch Street. The run-down nature of this area can clearly be seen in this 1949 view. Areas of derelict land abound as testament to the bombing that took place in the area in 1940 and 1941, with huge wooden props buttressing the walls of the surviving sub-standard buildings for a few more years. Compared to the photograph of car 728 on page 103, it will be noticed that the buildings at the end of Gooch Street, in this 1949 view, have been demolished. *R. T. Wilson*

Below On the last day of operation, a rather run-down and worn-out-looking car 418 passes through the equally run-down and worn-out Balsall Heath area. It is turning from Sherlock Street into St Lukes Road on the outward 37 route, entering a typical inner city area where the main roads tended to have commercial premises of a slightly better standard, often with ornate cornices, porched entrances and stone-faced brickwork, such as that on the corner behind the tram. However, once into the less prestigious roads, the quality of houses worsened, which, after 80 or more years of occupation, resulted in numerous areas in the city, including Balsall Heath, declining into squalor. Unfortunately the City Council could not afford to demolish them all at once, and throughout the early post-war period the Housing Department 'topped and tailed' houses that were basically unfit for human habitation in order to squeeze a few more years out of them. The western section of St Lukes Road to the left of the tram was an important bus route, used by the Inner Circle 8 route from 16 August 1926 until 27 September 1962, when it was diverted to cross Bristol Road at Belgrave Road. *A. K. Terry*

Top The mid-19th-century houses on the north side of St Lukes Road still had remnants of Regency styling in their street elevations, which contrasted with the later residences on the southern side. Car 363 sets down two passengers in the gas-lit road just beyond the junction to the left with Varna Road. This part of Balsall Heath near Pershore Road was known as St Martins, and was always regarded as being the 'better end' of the ward, being developed from about 1840 with 'exceedingly eligible villa residences'. The lands owned by the Moore family and that of the heirs of Rev Vincent Edwards in Balsall Heath were very quickly sold off for housing in increasingly small plots and increasingly spacious housing, comparing rather unfavourably with the controlled leasing of large plots in the nearby Calthorpe estate. The walls in front of the earlier houses to the right are later additions and have capping stones made of the famous Staffordshire blue brick. Today, with the exception of the distant school, all the buildings have gone, as has Varna Road, lost because of its reputation as the unofficial night-life centre of Birmingham! Even the name has been erased to expunge from the residents' minds its former seedy notoriety. *F. N. Lloyd Jones*

Middle Rather battered Brush-bodied bogie car 730, which entered service in December 1925 and is looking in need of a repaint and repair, prepares to move away after unloading its passengers in St Lukes Road at the junction of Belgrave Road during 1949. The late-Victorian house to the left, whose decorative brickwork can also be seen on the right of the next photograph, belonged to a later period of development than those behind the disembarking passengers. The whole area had been earmarked for redevelopment as early as 1942, although it would be nearly 20 years before the Highgate Comprehensive Development Scheme came to fruition. Car 730 is working on the 37 route to Cannon Hill; in common with most of Moseley Road depot's services, it opened on Tuesday 1 January 1907 and remained virtually unchanged for all of its 42-year life. *F. N. Lloyd Jones*

Bottom Working out of town in St Lukes Road in September 1949, car 366 is on the 39 route to Alcester Lanes End. Having just unloaded its passengers at Belgrave Road, it will travel straight across into Alexandra Road for about 200 yards before reaching the next junction at Balsall Heath Road. The Belgravia Hotel, behind the tram, in an already run-down and declining area, was hardly a centre of opulence and perhaps already being used by the first Commonwealth immigrants as

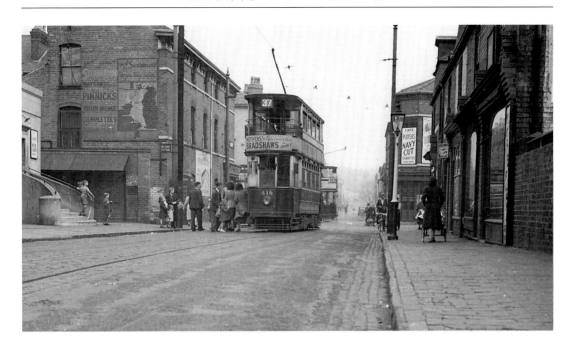

their first lodgings. As a tramcar due for withdrawal, 366 was transferred from Miller Street on 26 August 1949 to work out its last few weeks at Moseley Road depot, where it was broken up in October. *R. T. Wilson*

Above An interchange of passengers takes place on the Cannon Hill-bound, UEC-bodied, four-wheel car 418, outside the Luxor Cinema in Balsall Heath Road in 1949. Alongside the ornate exit of the cinema on the extreme left is an advertisement for the film *East Side of Heaven*, a treat that seems to be impressing no one, not least the two short-trousered boys. The cinema opened in November 1913 as the Balsall Heath Picture House, and

became the Luxor in the 1940s. It closed in 1983. Car 418 will turn hard right into Clevedon Road in front of the cafe; this is actually on the corner of Jakeman Walk, which diverged at the same point, and its building occupies the whole block up to the next road, Cox Street West. The intertwining tracks of 'the Chinese Railway' in this area were laid in adjacent streets with trams trundling up one narrow street, grinding around another tight turn and always going in only one direction. The rear of another 401 Class open-balconied car can be seen at the next crossroads, going into Longmore Street on its way into the city. *R. T. Wilson*

Above right In this pre-war view, UEC-built car 547 has reached the southern end of Clevedon Road at Jakeman Walk, and off to the left of picture is the entrance to

Calthorpe Park, opened on Whit Monday 1857 by HRH The Duke of Cambridge in front of a crowd of 100,000 people. The building behind the tram is the Calthorpe Works of glass merchants Parker & Osborn, destroyed in 1941. The similar 512 Class bogie car in the distance is also following the left-hand curve of Clevedon Road, while 547, on leaving this stop, will take the curve to the right and enter Court Road. As can be seen, most of the area at this junction was made up of mid-19th-century terraces, typically interspersed with factories. Car 547 entered service in 1913 and originally had open balconies. These were enclosed in July 1927 when the original Dick, Kerr KD19A 40hp motors were replaced with that company's DK30/1L 63hp motors. The tram saw service until the penultimate day of tramcar operation in the city in a service life of 39 years. *L. W. Perkins*

Above Milk was delivered by horse and cart in Birmingham until well into the 1950s. In 1949 one of the more extravagantly designed milk-floats stands with its apparently patient horse between the shafts on the corner of Court Road and Edward Road. Opposite, outside Jones's electrical shop, the hoarding advertises that Nat Jackley, the comedian well-known for his rubber-necked eccentric walk, is appearing in *Piccadilly Hayride* at the Birmingham Hippodrome, which car 365 would have passed on its way to Balsall Heath. As can be seen, the intending suburban tram passenger had the difficulty of having to walk into the road to board. Fortunately, with only the milk-float parked outside the public lavatories next door to the Cannon Hill public house and the Bradford van parked outside the electrical shop, there is little danger on this occasion. Car 365 will turn past the milk-float into Edward Road. *R. T. Wilson*

Below Four-wheel car 445 has stopped outside the Cannon Hill public house in order to let off the solitary, gabardine-coated chap, who kindly walked straight in front of the fleet number of the tram just as Ray Wilson pressed the shutter! The Court Road/Edward Road junction was served by both the 37 trams to Cannon Hill and the 39 route to Alcester Lanes End via Balsall Heath's 'Chinese Railway'. The 37 turned right into Cannon Hill Road, while 445 on the 39 route will swing left in front of the Cannon Hill pub and climb up Edward Road before turning right into Mary Street. Even by 1949 this part of Balsall Heath, only a stone's throw from Edgbaston Cricket Ground and the Calthorpe estate, was beginning to look down at heel. Woodward's grocery and provisions shop was typical of the backstreet shops in the days before supermarkets and more intensive consumer demands. If, in a row of suburban shops, there wasn't a fish and chip shop, there would be the 'caff', and a mug of tea, a 'cough and a drag' and a bacon sandwich in premises like the Windsor Cafe could brighten up even the grey-looking Balsall Heath! *R. T. Wilson*

Edward Road, the Cannon Hill loop and back to the city

Top The trams on the 37 service to Cannon Hill branched right at the end of Court Road and, on crossing Edward Road, turned into Cannon Hill Road. On 5 September 1949 car 728, in almost the same position as 365 pictured opposite, and with its upper saloon windows open, turns right at the triangular junction. In this view we can see more of the row of shops on the corner; one of them, Rawcliffe's, a newsagent and tobacconist, has three cigarette advertisements for 'Players Please' and one for Craven 'A'. In those far-off days, when nearly everyone smoked cigarettes, brand name advertising was not banned. *T. J. Edgington*

Middle By contrast, car 419, working the 39 route, has just turned left from Court Road into Edward Road and is passing Jakeman Road on the right. The straight line in the foreground, forming the third side of the triangle, was used for depot workings. The invalid carriage, fitted with a small motorcycle engine and therefore licensed and carrying a number plate, is parked outside the Cannon Hill Studio, a photographers whose portraits can be seen hanging in the window. The Edward Road area had a number of small shops and marked the boundary between the poorer-quality housing on the city side and the gradually improving quality towards Moseley; a photographer's studio here was thus not such a surprise. All these shops, like Hall's the ironmonger next door, with its galvanised dustbins and washing-tubs, would gradually disappear to be replaced by large supermarkets selling modern plastic equivalents. The tram will continue on the single-line track and turn second right into Mary Street, where for the first time since leaving Sherlock Street two-way working will recommence. *R. T. Wilson*

Bottom On Tuesday 10 June 1941 car 423 travels westwards along Edward Road towards Court Road at the Hallam Street junction, working the 37 route. Because of air raid damage it has been on a long detour via Leopold Street and Moseley Road, before turning into Edward Road along the tracks used for access to and from Moseley Road depot to regain Court Road, where it will turn left into Cannon Hill Road on its normal route just level with the approaching car. The tram is equipped with a complete set of wartime emergency features, including anti-blast mesh glued to the windows. *W. A. Camwell*

Above The single-line southbound working of the 37 route travelled for its last half-mile to the terminus round an anti-clockwise loop via Cannon Hill Road, having left the distant shops of Edward Road and entered the most residentially prestigious section of the route. This tree-lined area in Balsall Heath was developed at the very end of the 19th century; the bay-windowed terraced houses have small gardens, while decorative brickwork adorns their fronts. They echo the developments in nearby Moseley, being built to a grand scale with up to six bedrooms and large reception rooms with high ceilings, decorative architraves and ceiling roses. Car 418 trundles past the unconcerned children playing with their bicycles as an audience of older children surveys the general scene from the vantage of the tram's balcony. *R. T. Wilson*

Below The straight run down the 600 yards of Cannon Hill Road on the 37 route was crossed only once, at Willows Crescent, which, like the tram route, was lined with rather superior 1890s-built terraced housing. On a cold, sunny day

in 1943, car 440, adorned with all the usual accoutrements of wartime blackout requirements, stands at the last request stop in Cannon Hill Road during the period when the 37 only ran at peak periods, the all-day service having been withdrawn for economy reasons. Years before, this junction had been the location of a passing loop, but it was only ever occasionally used to park the odd tramcar near the 'back gate' of the nearby Warwickshire County Cricket Ground at Edgbaston, opened in 1886; although used as a test match venue during the Edwardian period, for most of the life of the 37 tram route test matches were rarely played there. The first was against Australia, and despite Wilfred Rhodes producing bowling figures of 7 for 17, resulting in the Aussies being all-out for 36, the match was drawn due to inclement weather. Only three other tests were played at Edgbaston in tram days, against Australia again in 1909, and in 1924 and 1929 against South Africa, producing two large wins and a draw. Test matches only returned to Edgbaston in 1957, some eight years after the Moseley Road tramway abandonment; in that first test against the West Indies, captain Peter May (285 not out) and Colin Cowdrey (154) put on 411 runs for the fourth wicket of the second innings; despite that, the match was drawn! *Author's collection*

Opposite top Car 415 stands at the compulsory stop at the junction of Cannon Hill Road and Edgbaston Road on a bleak wartime day in January 1943; like the tram, the street furniture also carries white blackout markings. It is perhaps slightly surprising that the 37 route, which realistically was little more than a large loop off the 'main-line'

service through Balsall Heath, as retained during the war. The 37 service finished its outward run by turning left into Edgbaston Road and, after passing the entrance to Cannon Hill Park, arrived at the terminus in Willows Road; about 50 yards away to the left is the culverted River Rea, which flows behind the stands of the Edgbaston cricket ground. *Burrows Brothers*

Middle It is amazing how many times the fleet number of a tram is obscured on commercial postcards! Lamp standards, cyclists or pedestrians are quite common, but the most regular offenders are the crews themselves – they seem to delight in having a conversation when standing right in front of the car, usually at the terminus, but always in the middle of the road! A therefore unidentifiable member of the 1926 702 Class stands at the terminus in Willows Road in about 1935. The purpose of the postcard is to show the new traffic island at the junction of Edgbaston Road and Russell Road (in the foreground); the Belisha beacons, first introduced in 1934, were put in place at about the same time, to discourage pedestrians from crossing the junction via the roundabout. *Commercial postcard*

THE TRAFFIC CONTROL EDGBASTON RD ᵛ RUSSELL RD. EDGBASTON

Bottom The Willows Road terminus was an interesting urban boundary between the small Victorian terraced artisans housing and back-to-back courtyards that characterised much of Balsall Heath and the larger villas built for the white-collar workers in Moseley and Kings Heath. From its junction with Willows Crescent as far as Edgbaston Road, the houses in Willows Road were larger and of better quality, as exemplified by the big bay windows of the house next to car 444. Looking from the tram stop across the traffic island seen above, more large houses for the professional and business people of late-Victorian Birmingham can be seen, though in distant Russell Road the prime sites overlooking Cannon Hill Park were not developed until the inter-war period. Car 444 is in its full wartime garb in the early part of 1941; note the little post-box-sized strips in the window blackout material through which passengers would hopefully see where they were at night. *C. C. Thornburn collection*

Top Bogie car 725 is standing at the terminus in Willows Road by the Bundy clock, which incidentally had various positions there. It is late September 1949 and the Cannon Hill route has only a few days to run before being replaced

indirectly by the 48 bus service; this would not use the one-way system in the same way as the trams, which left a number of streets on the so-called 'Chinese Railway' devoid of a bus service. *Lens of Sutton*

Middle Recently repainted Cotteridge bogie car 830 was used on Sunday 10 July 1949, together with Miller Street four-wheeler 367, to operate an LRTL tour of the Birmingham system. It is seen here turning from Lincoln Street into Edward Road using the curve installed in 1919 for depot workings only. The tracks in the foreground are the inbound ones in Hallam Street from the 37 route terminus in Willows Road, which car 830 had used before starting this manoeuvre. Normal service trams working the 37 route continued along Lincoln Street, made famous for many years by the Ford car agency, Lincoln Street Motors, whose showrooms were situated there. At the next junction, opposite the trees just visible in the distance, was Balfour Street, where the inbound Alcester Lanes End cars on the 39 group of routes rejoined the Cannon Hill trams on their return journey to the city. *A. N. H. Glover*

Bottom Returning to the 39 route outbound bogie car 728 turns from Edward Road into Mary Street working towards Alcester Lanes End towards the end of its 26-month sojourn at Moseley Road depot which started at the beginning of September 1947. The tracks going straight over the junction just in front of 728 were used by Balsall Heath trams to access Moseley Road depot; passengers were allowed on these depot workings, although not on official fare-paying journeys. The Hillman in the background is the only post-war vehicle to be seen while gas lamps like that on the left remained throughout the city until the mid-1960s. The buildings that included George Le Resche's Balsall Heath Motors were swept away in the Balsall Heath redevelopments of the 1970s. *R. T. Wilson*

Opposite above Looking run-down and shabby in the summer of 1949, inbound car 416 has descended Mary Street working on the 39 route and has stopped at the compulsory red stop before crossing Edward Road in the foreground. It is outside the Regency Dry Cleaners and barely

ts a second glance from the three young women and the tle boy in the pram. The opposite side of Mary Street, hind the photographer, was one of the earlier velopments in Balsall Heath, with some small orkshops and 11 houses being recorded in the 1841 nsus. Gradually the road and its associated buildings read to the south up the hill towards Edgbaston Road d Park Road beyond, and the nature of the housing anged, becoming purely residential, and generally of o storeys. *R. T. Wilson*

elow The serried terraces of Victorian houses in Mary Street gave way to a strange group just north of Edgbaston Road. The seven houses to the left, on the sharp descent to the Strensham Road junction, which bogie car 717 is approaching, were built with wrought-iron-balustraded balconies separated by delicate trelliswork. They look a little the worse for wear here, but have since been restored and survive today. By way of contrast, the dismal row of three-storey houses and shops opposite leading to the junction with Edgbaston Road have all been demolished. Car 717, working the 39 route, is passing the cross-over where the 49 route trams turned back. *F. N. Lloyd Jones*

Below City of Birmingham Tramways' Kitson Steam Locomotive No 73, built in 1894, is running firebox-first while towing one of the first series of Falcon canopy-topped, double-deck bogie trailers; built in 1884, they were the only ones to have knifeboard seating in the open-sided upper saloon. The trailer is displaying the route letter 'K', signifying that it is working on the Kings Heath via Balsall Heath route. This was opened in July 1886 by the Birmingham Central Tramways Company; the steam trams operated from Hill Street and their route was largely followed by the replacement Corporation electric trams that took over on 1 January 1907. Alternate journeys normally turned back at the Edward Road-Mary Street junction and would display the destination letter 'B'. On this sunny summer's day, probably around the turn of the 19th century, the ensemble of loco and trailer stands in Park Road at the loop at Augusta Road. *M. Rooum*

Bottom Car 448 has worked 'the Chinese Railway' on the 39 route through Balsall Heath and is emerging from Park

Road into Alcester Road in 1949; the top of the climb up Mary Street can be seen behind the tram. This junction was dominated by the large Victorian house that stood in its own grounds on the corner on the right, representing the largest type of late-19th-century development when Moseley vied with Edgbaston as the most prestigious address around Birmingham. Although the house has recently been demolished, much of this area remains the same today, its properties, which a few years ago looked decidedly worn out, being renovated and gentrified. The tram will continue through Moseley Village and on to the Alcester Lanes End terminus some 2 miles away (see page 116). *R. T. Wilson*

Right A Daimler COG5 bus speeds past along Moseley Road as the driver of 1925 Brush-built bogie car 719 uses his point-bar to alter the points at the end of Edward Road on Friday 26 August 1949 to enable the tram to right into Moseley Road and return to the depot. The tram has been recently repainted and is in sparkling condition, although the cast-iron blue and orange enamel plate advertisement for Dewar's whisky looks as if it has a fair amount of rust near the gutter drainage pipe, but then it may be more than 20 years old. The late-1940s equivalent of Mothercare is advertised on the tram – 'After the Stork – Little Toddlers' – but this appears to be a paper advertisement. Car 719 moved to Miller Street on 10 September 1949, some three weeks before the abandonment, together with cars 716 and 721, to be replaced by 301 Class four-wheelers 339, 365 and 366, which were exhibiting signs of ageing and were due for withdrawal. The latter ran out their time at Moseley Road, releasing the bogie cars on a one-for-one basis. *T. J. Edgington*

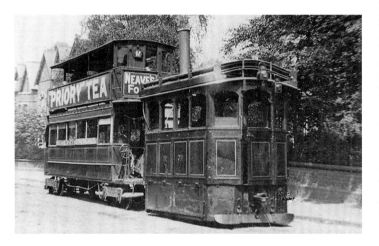

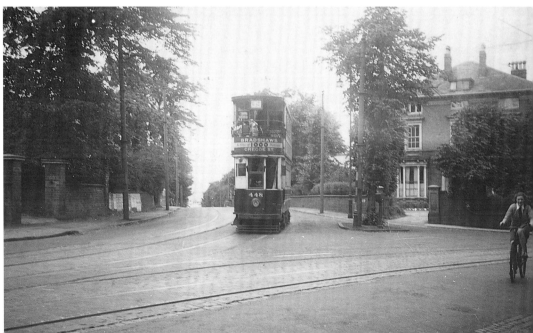

Above right Car 438 is on its way into the city in Balfour Street; it has just turned left from Mary Street in the distance, and is about to take the right-hand curve into Lincoln Street, where it will join the incoming cars on the 37 route via Cox Street West. It has already travelled 200 yards from Edward Road on the tortuous Balsall Heath inbound line and has over half a mile to go before rejoining the outbound tracks in Sherlock Street. The close-knit communities that developed in areas like Balsall Heath almost made up for the housing conditions, where typically as many as 90 per cent of properties lacked indoor sanitation, and bathrooms were virtually unheard of – yet it was considered 'quite nice' to live in a two-up, two-down terraced house. The public baths, opened in Moseley Road in 1906 and built in the Flemish-Jacobean style favoured for many public utility buildings in Edwardian Birmingham, meant that often cleanliness was only a tram-ride away. *F. N. Lloyd Jones*

Right Meanwhile, on inbound route 37, car 728 passes perhaps the last trees on its way in from the sylvan delights of nearby Cannon Hill. It is in Lincoln Street, and at the distant three-storey corner shop will fork left into Cox Street West. The sunny day cannot disguise the years of neglect and decay in this part of Balsall Heath. All would be swept away in the comprehensive redevelopment programme of the 1960s, which removed for ever roads like Cox Street West, which was named after a land-owning family in the area who could trace their ancestry back to 1608 when the area had been poor-quality farmland. Ironically, today grassed open spaces cover large tracts of Balsall Heath, so the land use has gone almost full circle in nearly 400 years. *F. N. Lloyd Jones*

Below In the background of the photograph of car 418 outside the Luxor Cinema in Balsall Heath Road (page 93) can be seen an open-balconied tram going on its inward journey. Here, car 731 is about to perform the same manoeuvre, crossing Balsall Heath Road from Cox Street West into Longmore Street beneath the stylishly embellished block of shops, the corner one having the large number 79 on it, visible above the tram. In the earlier photograph the same embellished frieze below the eaves can be seen. The return route to the city altered noticeably from this point: the unending terraces of houses gave way to rows of small shops nearly all the way to the Sherlock Street junction almost half a mile away. *F. N. Lloyd Jones*

Bottom left Having just crossed Belgrave Road from Longmore Street, Brush car 726 travels along the 50 or so yards from the junction in Gooch Street before taking the curve into the straight 600-yard main section of the route that will take it to Sherlock Street. It is 1949 and the tram is in the last style of livery. The reputation of the 'Brummie' with his flat accent, dry sense of humour and hard-working but unimaginative nature might also be applied to the trams. Elsewhere, tram classes and designs were given interesting names, like Liverpool's 'Cabin Cars' and 'Green Goddesses', and Glasgow's 'Coronations' and 'Cunarders', while all Belfast trams built after 1920 were named after the general manager responsible for their construction, a tradition followed for a time in Leeds. In Birmingham odd trams were given names: cars 451 and 452 were known as the 'Titanics' and 342 was the 'Armoured Car', then there were the 'Peckhams' and the 'Brill-Maleys' and, of course, the 'Lightweights', 842 and 843, but they were hardly names to conjure with! Yet here is car 726, one of a fairly substantial order of 30 built by Brush in 1925, known within the Tramways Department as '32Hs'! *F. N. Lloyd Jones*

Below Having turned sharp left in Gooch Street, the trams went though a shopping area consisting of small family concerns or local chains of shops such as the Wrensons grocery chain. Car 716 passes on the left a Birmingham-registered Austin Seven of 1937 vintage parked facing in the wrong direction, while on the other side of Gooch Street is a Morris Eight. The tram has worked in from Cannon Hill and is at the junction with Hope Street. The Gooch Street route had originally been constructed by the Birmingham Central Tramways Company as a steam tram service, opened on 19 July 1886 through Balsall Heath and joining up with the Moseley Road service. *F. N. Lloyd Jones*

Above At the city end of Gooch Street, at the junction with Sherlock Street, inbound trams from Balsall Heath and Cannon Hill turned right and crossed the 'out of city' lines. This view of the junction shows the corner buildings before demolition (see page 91). Bogie car 728 is about to leave the compulsory stop in Gooch Street and is passing a police telephone kiosk on the corner. The only building from this era left here today is the public house on the corner of Gooch Street and Barford Street. *R. T. Wilson*

Moor Street to Moseley Road

Below Open-balconied, four-wheel car 441, built in 1912 by UEC, passes the mock-Tudor-fronted Atkinson's public house, The Corner, as it turns from Moor Street into Carrs

Lane in the summer of 1949. It is a 40hp-motored tram mounted on 7ft 6in Mountain & Gibson trucks and belongs to the 50-strong 401 Class; these looked very similar to the preceding 361 Class, although they were considerably heavier as they were fitted with the air and oil brake. Tram 441 has turned just ahead of an inbound Coventry Road trolleybus belonging to the 17-66 Class of Leyland TTBD2 six-wheelers, and will inch its way past a 1949 Daimler CVG6 on the 37 route to Hall Green and 1948 Daimler CVD6 1790 (HOV 790), which is picking up passengers for the 44 service. Beyond that bus in another Leyland six-wheel trolleybus working the 94 route. Unlike the Daimler COG5 seen at the far end of Carrs Lane, tram 441 will twice turn right; first into High Street, then into Albert Street outside the Beehive store. *R. T. Wilson*

Top Car 403 is also turning into Carrs Lane at The Corner public house in 1949 before making its way up towards High Street, working the 42 route. The tram will have dropped most of its passengers off at the Bull Ring end of Moor Street as, at this time, the markets area was easily accessible; the later road system left the Bull Ring Centre and associated markets very isolated from access by public transport. This was the Achilles' heel of the 1960s redevelopment of the traditional market centre of Birmingham, leading to the widespread recent redevelopment of the impressive new Bullring Centre. Car 403 shows the traditional nature of these trams. They were the last four-wheel cars to be purchased new by BCT in 1912, yet when built they were at the forefront of tramcar development; the subsequent 512 Class of bogie cars, also constructed by UEC, which were built the following year, were only 4-foot-longer versions of the same basic open-balconied design. *F. N. Lloyd Jones*

Middle Carrs Lane was an important focus of public transport in Birmingham's city centre, being used by routes coming in from the south and south-eastern sides of the city. The trams and trolleybuses turned right into High Street, then right again to their termini in Albert Street before leaving the city centre via another right turn back into Moor Street. Empty car 444, on the short-working 50 route from Trafalgar Road, leads Leyland TTBD2 six-wheel trolleybus 48 (OC 1148) past the imposing Town Mills warehouse as they climb Carrs Lane towards High Street. Behind the second trolleybus is a similar procession, with car 441 and trolleybus 35 (OC 1135) leading a Daimler COG5 that is negotiating the Moor Street turn outside The Corner public house (as seen above). The derelict site on the right, used for parking cars, was created on the night of 9-10 April 1941 when a force of 250 bombers dropped 650 high-explosive bombs and 170 sets of incendiaries on the city. This destroyed many buildings in the High Street and New Street area, including these in Carrs Lane, and killed or injured some 1,121 people throughout the city. *R. T. Wilson*

Bottom On a miserable Sunday 17 July 1949, car 402 approaches the top of Carrs Lane when working on the 42 route and passes the interwar-built Broderick's bedding and furniture store before turning right into High

Street. Standing opposite Carrs Lane is Hilton's clothes store, one of the few early-19th-century buildings in this part of the city to escape the bombing raids of 1940 and 1941. By way of contrast, 402 has on its balcony dash an advertisement for E. R. Green, a ladies' coat and dress shop in Kings Heath, which would outlast Broderick's, Hilton's and the tramcar by at least 30 years. *C. C. Thornburn*

Right This fine study of car 389 as it turns from High Street into Albert Street, in front of the RAF recruitment office on the first floor and the Corner House confectionery shop, shows it still in the pre-war lined-out livery. The delicate wrought-ironwork on the open balcony seems at odds with the rest of the functional design; the open balcony was necessary because of the Board of Trade's refusal to allow the operation of narrow-gauge, totally enclosed, four-wheel, double-deck tramcars. These 301 Class cars were among the first in the country, when built in 1912, to be fitted with Dick, Kerr DK13A 40hp motors and Preston 'flexible axle' swing-yoke 7ft 6in-wheelbase trucks. They were also lower than any preceding Birmingham trams, being only 15ft 7½in high, enabling them to pass beneath the low bridges at Aston Station and Selly Oak. Car 389 continued in service until the closure of the Moseley Road trams on 1 October 1949 and was broken up at Moseley Road depot in December of that year. *F. N. Lloyd Jones*

Below UEC four-wheeled, open-balcony car 363 was allocated to Moseley Road depot from October 1948 until September 1949. The depot's normal allocation of four-wheelers was the similar-looking 401 Class, but from early in the Second World War there were always between four and six of the ubiquitous 301 Class allocated there. The tram is crossing into Dale End before turning back into Martineau Street on a Villa Park special in the winter of 1948-49, and is passing in front of the subterranean gentlemen's lavatory at the bottom of Bull Street. It is attended by two members of the BCT Inspectorate, one in the foreground in front of the Washwood Heath bogie

tram standing in Dale End and the other seemingly 'walking' 363 over the cross-over. The policeman on point duty seems to have the attention of the pedestrians, but standing as he is at the bottom of Martineau Street, next to the temporary buildings on the bomb-site, he appears not to be involved in the trams' manoeuvres. Behind 363 in High Street is a Coventry Road six-wheel trolleybus and a Daimler CVD6 of 1948 vintage working the recently introduced 54 route from Stechford. *F. N. Lloyd Jones*

Top The principal service from the city centre to Alcester Lanes End was numbered 42, but it had numerous short-workings. Here car 448 stands at the impressive shelters in Albert Street outside the Beehive, an independent department store advertising itself as 'A Warehouse for the People'. It sold everything from household goods to baby clothes, and for many years retained its wonderful overhead cable system whereby small brass canisters were sent to a central point in the store where all payments and change were dealt with. After many years of contraction and struggle, the Beehive closed on Leap Year Day 1972, having been in business for just over a century. Car 448 is seen on Saturday 10 September 1949 in company with Daimler COG5 bus 1057 (CVP 157), built in 1937 and one of 41 such pre-war buses that would survive until 1960. It is working on the 54 route to Stechford, which itself had only been introduced 11 months earlier when the 84 tram service had been abandoned. *F. N. Lloyd Jones*

Middle After leaving the Albert Street terminus, the Moseley Road trams turned back into Moor Street. Just before the former Great Western Railway station of that name, traffic had to negotiate the rise in the ground as the road passed over the 596-yard railway tunnel carrying the railway from the south to Snow Hill Station on the other side of the city centre. Car 403 crests the rise in Moor Street when working towards the Bull Ring on the 42 route in the early part of 1949. *F. N. Lloyd Jones*

Bottom On its way to Kyotts Lake Road on Saturday 4 July 1953 is Brush totally enclosed GEC WT32H 40hp bogie car 728, which had been one of Moseley Road depot's allocation until 1 October 1949 when it was transferred to Miller Street. It is seen here making its last journey to the works for scrapping, and was one of 23 cars to be broken up in the early part of August 1953. Towering above the surrounding buildings is Moor Street Warehouse, owned by the family concern of A. J. Norton. After 50 years of trading it closed in March 1964 and the building was destroyed in a fire on 14 August 1965; this was the worst fire in the city since the Halfords blaze ten years earlier, and needed 100 firemen and 23 appliances to control it. The tram is passing Moor Street Station, opened by the GWR on 1 July 1909 to help relieve Snow Hill of the increasing burden of commuter traffic on the lines from Leamington Spa and Stratford-upon-Avon. The station had a pleasant if unassuming entrance that lacked the grandeur and romance of Snow Hill and the sheer size of New Street, and always looked an uncomfortable adjunct to the transport system of Birmingham; its glazed bricks and little kiosks were an Edwardian delight, and would have been much more at home in a smaller town. The station was replaced on Monday 28 September 1987, but with the help of Chiltern Trains and Birmingham Council it has been beautifully restored as a working Edwardian station. *T. J. Edgington*

Top right On the same wet Sunday as seen on the page 104, 17 July 1949, four-wheel car 420 speeds up Moor Street going eastwards over the railway tunnel working the 42 route. In the distance is the Woolworth building on the other side of the Bull Ring in Spiceal Street. Car 420 will soon turn left into Carrs Lane in order to reach its terminus in Albert Street. This air and oil brake car retained its pre-war livery until withdrawal on the last day of

operation on 1 October 1949. After a 37-year service life at Moseley Road depot it would be broken up there in December of that year by George Cohen & Son Ltd.

Moor Street was one of Birmingham's oldest streets and the name is a corruption of 'moledum', meaning a mill. In fact, a mill existed in the area up to the end of the 17th century, and after that the road became important as a routeway below the hill on which the centre of Birmingham stood, linking the southern routes into the city with those leading out to Aston and the Tame valley. The mid-19th-century shops behind the tram survived until the late 1950s when the Inner Ring Road Scheme, inspired by Herbert Manzoni, swept them away, leaving only a small section of the original route fronting Moor Street Station extant. *C. C. Thornburn*

Above right The Bull Ring was the area between Moor Street, on the extreme left of this 1949 view, and Park Street, approximately where the M&B public house on the skyline is situated. Until emasculated by the 1960s redevelopment, it was the spiritual and historical centre of Birmingham. In 2003, although now a totally pedestrianised area, a new Bullring was opened as one of the most prestigious shopping centres in Europe. Always the city's traditional market place, it traces its origins back

to the Domesday Book, when the original settlement of Birmingham on this site was worth 20 shillings. To the right is the parish church of St Martin, one of Birmingham's main medieval buildings, being first mentioned in 1263, but rebuilt between 1873 and 1875 by the versatile local architect, J. A. Chatwin. He earned a reputation for being 'thorough but uninspired' as far as his Gothic rebuilding of churches was concerned. St Martin's, with its imposing tower, stands today as an ecclesiastical and architectural focus over the market area of the city.

Car 414, one of four of the 401 Class with extended UEC trucks of 8ft 6in wheelbase, turns out of Moor Street on the 42 route and passes 1949 Midland Red BMMO FEDD 1865 (HOV 865) parked in front of St Martin's; its rather uninformative destination blind shows that this Daimler CVG6 is on its way to the Hall Green terminus, working over the route of the former 17 tram route, abandoned some 12 years previously. The tram is about the descend the Bull Ring on its way to Digbeth and the turn into Rea Street, and is being met by similar UEC four-wheel car 443, preceding Leyland six-wheeled trolleybus 24 (OC 1124) working into Albert Street from Coventry Road on the 94 route. It will be seen that the tram is using the common positive wire of the trolleybus overhead. *R. T. Wilson*

Top On a bright summer's day in 1949, car 415, painted in the 1946-style livery, descends the Bull Ring on the 42 route. It has turned out of Moor Street, on the corner of which stands the impressive early-19th-century building occupied by the Oswald Bailey Army & Navy Stores, and behind it is the upper part of the Bull Ring. In this bustling heart of Birmingham was a whole range of shops that carried on down the hill into Spiceal Street. Opposite the Midland Red utility bus in the distance, dwarfing the shops, stood the huge Market Hall built in 1833 to the design of Charles Edge. This received a direct hit by incendiaries in an air raid on 25 August 1940, but for the next 23 years the roofless shell continued to serve as a market. For many years two disarmed German bombs stood on plinths and served as collection points for various charities until the building was demolished in January 1964. The whole of this area was in dire need of redevelopment after further ravages of war and in the early 1960s was completely swept away by the Bull Ring Centre and the Inner Ring Road. *F. N. Lloyd Jones*

Middle In the lined-out pre-war livery, four-wheeled car 420, one of the 50-strong 401 Class built in 1912 by UEC, stands at the tram stop at the Digbeth-Meriden Street junction, just beyond the elaborately styled Digbeth police station. It is working the 42 route to Alcester Lanes End and, after passing the garage with the semi-circular gable front beyond the Morris Eight car, will turn right into Rea Street before eventually gaining the main Moseley Road route. Car 420 received its last repaint in September 1945 and was withdrawn on 1 October 1949, not long after this picture was taken. *C. Carter*

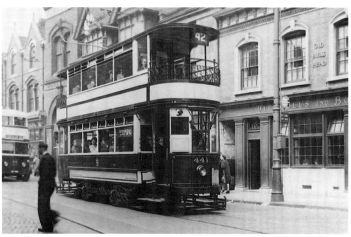

Bottom Car 441 stands in Digbeth outside M&B's Old Bull's Head public house, about to turn right into Rea Street on the 42 route to Alcester Lanes End. The following Leyland TTBD2 MCCW-bodied trolleybus on the 92 route still has a cream roof; all bus roofs were painted a muddy brown during the Second World War, and a modified light shade of khaki was retained after the end of hostilities as it was harder-wearing than the original all-over cream. Therefore this is a pre-war view, showing that the UEC-bodied four-wheeler, even after over 20 years of service, is in remarkably good condition. The Old Bull's Head survived the road-widening and redevelopment of the 1950s and is still a hostelry today. On the traction pole on the right is the Selector Relay Switch box, which connected the actuating mechanism between the overhead-line switch and the points on the track for trams going into Rea Street. Also on the traction pole is one of the hexagonal trolleybus stops, just above the oblong tram stop. *W. J. Haynes*

Right Digbeth in about 1935 was a narrow bustling thoroughfare into which funnelled all the tram routes going towards the Bull Ring: the Stratford and Warwick Road routes, the Coventry Road and Stechford services and those Moseley Road routes that started from Albert Street. Car 433 is working on the 50 route short-working to Moseley Road and the depot, and is just passing Digbeth Civic Hall on the right. It will shortly turn right and follow the Midland Red single-decker into Rea Street. The tram is being followed by what appears to be a Brush-bodied AEC Regent 661 of 1929. In the distance, at the rear of a queue of trams waiting to cross the Moat Row-Meriden Street junction, is Leyland TTBD2 six-wheeled trolleybus 35 (OC 1135), working on the 92 route to Albert Street. The tall, grime-encrusted buildings on the left separated Digbeth from Midland Red's Digbeth garage, and when these properties were cleared the site was used as a hard-standing for that company's buses for a number of years until the mid-1950s. *Author's collection*

Below The Digbeth end of Rea Street was very run-down after years of neglect. A pre-war road-widening scheme was frozen for nearly 20 years, which contributed to the planning blight in the area. Interestingly, however, the buildings that were cleared to enable Digbeth/Deritend to become a dual-carriageway did not include the garage advertising overhauls, seen just behind the tram. This site is still awaiting development, although during the summer months it is occasionally used as an overspill car park for coaches using the Digbeth coach station. Car 431, approaching the city on the 42 route, had something of an unusual early career. It ran as a single-decker, initially as 'The Committee Car' for the Birmingham Tramways Committee and subsequently as a single-deck tractor pulling ex-CBT car 509 on the Nechells route. After this continental-inspired trailer operation ended, car 431 was fitted with a BCT-built top-cover at Kyotts Lake Road Works in May 1923. This upper saloon was not built with top-light windows, which made the car easy to identify as the only member of the class so fitted. It had the dubious distinction of operating the last car on the 41 route via Leopold Street on the final night, Saturday 1 October 1949. *Author's collection*

Below Rea Street, where the trams passed the Midland Red bus garage, was the link between the tracks in Digbeth and those in Bradford Street. The garage had opened on 3 July 1929 and gradually became the largest of Midland Red's garages, having an allocation of more than 120 buses. The Digbeth area of Birmingham was the original crossing point of the River Rea, which flows behind the mainly Victorian shops and factories fronting the south-eastern side of the street. Although obviously having seen better days, the street's character – small factory units mixed with warehouses and specialised shops – did produce a rich and lively feel to this heart of industrial Birmingham. UEC oil and air brake car 444 is working on the 42 route to Alcester Lanes End on 19 March 1949. It has its own overhead separate from the Coventry Road to Station Street trolleybuses, and this complicated overhead wiring was to survive the closure of the Moseley Road tram routes on 1 October 1949 to serve the 93 trolleybus service that ran until the last day of June 1951. The tram lines remained wired up until the final closure to enable tramcars to be transferred to and from Kyotts Lake Road Works off Stratford Road. *A. Yates*

Bottom Car 406 turns from Bradford Street into Rea Street in front of the Anchor Inn on 24 July 1949, a pub that in recent years has won numerous local CAMRA awards. It is painted in the post-war livery, in which nearly all of this class were repainted. Although with only just over two months service left, it looks in good condition. In the background, at the far end of Bradford Street, is the impressive Smithfield market on the corner of Moat Row and Moat Lane, designed by the then Borough Surveyor, W. Spooner Till, in 1883. It had round-arched lower-floor windows and well-designed wrought-iron main gates set in red-brick walls. This huge Victorian building stood on the site of the medieval manor house belonging to the de Bermingeham family, and was eventually demolished. *G. F. Douglas*

Opposite top Once the Moseley Road cars were in Bradford Street they were faced with a half-mile straight run out of the Rea valley. Built in the 1770s, the street was named after a landlord of the time, one Henry Bradford, a timber merchant and prominent Quaker, who lived in Old Square, and linked the turnpikes coming into Birmingham from the south with the market area around Moat Row, just below the Bull Ring. It had once been a drovers' route into the then enlarging town, accounting for its

straightness and width. Later, the 19th-century growth in industrial development in the Digbeth and Deritend area somewhat altered the urban structure of the area and it became one of Birmingham's major industrial areas. Yet despite the area's dramatic change from agriculture to heavy industry, the road itself retained its original wide character. Car 442, working on the 42 route, has just descended Bradford Street and is about to turn right into Rea Street. This particular car was one of only 23 of the 401-450 Class to be fitted with the quieter helical gears. *A. Yates*

Middle At the top of the steep climb up Bradford Street, the Moseley Road trams turned right into Moseley Road itself. Turning out of Moseley Road with a full load, in front of the Shepherds Rest public house, is car 407, one of the usual UEC-bodied, Mountain & Gibson four-wheel-truck cars, fitted with the Spencer-Dawson air and oil brake and one of only three cars in the class to receive the final plain-style numerals at both ends. The Shepherds Rest was a most aptly named hostelry, with Bradford Street's origin as a drovers' route. Certainly, as late as the 1870s animals that had been driven to market were penned up in Bradford Street before being consigned to the abattoir. At the bottom of the street, adjacent to the markets, was the Drovers' Arms. *R. T. Wilson*

Bottom On 20 August 1949 car 729, one of the Brush-built GEC 40hp '32H' Class bogie cars, turns into Moseley Road on the 42 route. The tram had been assembled in 1925 at Moseley Road depot, and within two years, in common with the rest of the 702-731 Class, was allocated to that depot. With the wholesale redistribution of cars that occurred after the Hockley abandonment on 2 April 1939, the entire class went either to Miller Street or Witton. On the night of 4 December 1940 nine of the class were so severely damaged that they never ran again after the roof of Witton depot collapsed on them; ironically, all nine were stored for the duration of the Second World War at Moseley Road. One further tram, 771, was destroyed in April 1941 during an air raid on Miller Street after a further re-sorting of the tram fleet caused by the Ladywood abandonment. Tram 729 survived until the final Erdington closure of 4 July 1953, and is seen here,

freshly painted, among the mixed Victorian industrial and residential frontages that characterised the Moseley Road area. *T. J. Edgington*

Below The true run-down squalor of the three-storey back-to-back terraces of inner Birmingham can be seen here in Moseley Road. The tunnel entries alternating with the front doors usually led to a courtyard behind with communal lavatories, water pumps and wash-houses. The back-to-backs that faced the street gave a false indication of artisan prosperity, with their embellishments of entablatures and architraves. This was a reminder of the days when Victorian entrepreneurial landowners squeezed as many properties as possible on to their land in order to make as much profit from the investment. Construction of back-to-back housing became illegal under the 1870 Housing Act, and in Birmingham at least, unlike Leeds for example, such appallingly mean housing was succeeded by the later, better-quality tunnel-back terraces. Car 412, working the 48 route in 1949, makes its way past these dismal rows of houses, which survived until the 1950s, just short of the junction with Bradford Street. Travelling along Bradford Street in the distance is a Daimler COG5 with a BRCW body going into the city on one of the Stratford Road services. *F. N. Lloyd Jones*

Bottom The post-war dereliction caused by bombing left Moseley Road with a number of abandoned areas of waste-ground. Car 438 is seen meeting identical car 424 at the Moseley Street junction in 1949, and has just passed the entrance of Highgate Park to the left of the picture. This opened on 2 June 1876 and had the unfortunate distinction of receiving more than 200 bombs during the war. Opposite the park and to the right of the photograph were built some gracious and impressive houses for Birmingham's manufacturers who saw the Highgate area as a haven from the nearby smoky, industrial areas that gave them their wealth. *R. T. Wilson*

Opposite top Just visible in Stratford Place is the early-17th-century timber-framed and plaster-walled Stratford House. Built in 1601 for Ambrose Rotton and his wife Bridget, it is a typical Warwickshire farmhouse of the period of a sort that would have been built by a prosperous yeoman. That it survived the subsequent enclosures and the gradual urban growth of the Balsall Heath area in the early 19th century is extremely surprising. The land immediately behind the house was used for the Birmingham & Gloucester Railway's passenger terminus from 17 December 1840, and later became the Midland Railway's goods yard. A single tram line off Stratford Place ran into Camp Hill goods station, as it was from here that permanent way material such as ballast, granite paving-blocks and cement were transported to the BCT tramway system. Indeed, the 702-731 Class were delivered to Camp Hill from Loughborough by the Brush Company between September 1925 and January 1926; the upper and lower saloons were transported separately and the two halves were hauled along Moseley Road by horse-drawn low-loaders to the depot for

assembly. Car 417 trundles between the large advertising hoarding and the Austin K2 furniture removal van on a winter's day in 1948 on its way out of the city. *D. Sanders collection*

Middle Once the trams left Stratford Place on the 42, 48 and 50 routes from Bradford Street, they met the 40 and 41 routes that arrived at Moseley Road from Hill Street terminus via the steep hill in Leopold Street. Car 416, one of Moseley Road depot's UEC-bodied, 54-seat, 40hp four-wheelers mounted on Mountain & Gibson 7ft 6in trucks, passes the junction of Moseley Road and Leopold Street on 17 September 1949, just a fortnight before all the Moseley Road group of routes were abandoned. It is carrying a fairly full load despite its down-at-heel state: the far-end dash panel has a large dent in it and the condition of the paintwork shows that it is some four years since the tram's last repaint. Thirty-four of the 50 cars of the 401 Class were repainted between September 1946 and February 1949, leaving the remainder, including 416, to soldier on in an increasingly deteriorating state. *T. J. Edgington*

Bottom The cobbled road surfaces of our major cities are today just a memory, but for normal vehicular traffic at the time of this photograph, September 1949, they were a major source of wear and tear to the suspension, which was constantly flexed as the surface was not flat but often rose and fell in a series of sickening lurches. When wet the setts became an ideal surface on which to practise the art of skid control. Finally, there was the incessant drumming through the tyres. An early post-war Austin 10 waits behind tram 366, wearing the pre-war livery. Ahead, car 329, the only tram at that time in Moseley Road's allocation not to carry advertisements, stands just before the junction with Leopold Street. Car 434, approaching from the other direction on the 41 route, was one of the few members of the 1912-built 401 Class to be modified, being temporarily fitted with a Brush truck in May 1920 and subsequently an extended version of the standard

Mountain & Gibson truck with an 8ft 6in wheelbase. Although we are only about a quarter of a mile from the appalling properties near Bradford Street, the quality of the housing built in the third quarter of the 19th century improved enormously with the out-of-city spread of two-up, two-down terraces. *R. T. Wilson*

Top Working the city-bound 42 route, car 387 fills up with passengers in Moseley Road just north of the Highgate Road/Belgrave Road junction. The distant advertisement is for Swallow raincoats, and it was at that point, at Montpelier Street, that the passenger entrance to the down side of Camp Hill railway station was situated. The pre-war Morris 10cwt van parked just beyond the road junction appears to be delivering to the newsagent and tobacconist shop beyond Lloyds Bank, which was on the Highgate Road corner; the newsagent seems to be attracting more window-shoppers than customers on this cold, sunny afternoon in early 1949. Tram 387 was one of only a very few to escape the mass breaking-up of Moseley Road's allocation when its routes were abandoned, being transferred to Witton depot on 16 September 1949 and surviving for another year. *F. N. Lloyd Jones*

Middle Moseley Road rarely allowed for any really fast running until beyond Kings Heath, but the section between Belgrave Road and Edward Road did allow for a burst of speed. The open-balconied 401 Class were only equipped with 40hp Dick, Kerr DK13A motors, but a spirited ride could be taken on sections of street track such as this. Car 442 had been fitted with Hoffman axle roller-bearings in December 1945, which gave the car a smoother, quieter and slightly faster ride. It is just about to pass a 1939 Huddersfield-registered Ford Prefect parked on the corner of Lime Grove opposite Balsall Heath baths and library. Just visible above the tram through the trees is the decorated west tower of St Paul's church, a Gothic-styled building consecrated in 1853 and pulled down in the 1980s, a decade that also saw the construction of Haden Way, part of the Middle Ring Road Scheme. This diverted the line of the main road into the city away from Moseley Road behind the buildings to the left of this view. In the far distance, coming from the Belgrave Road traffic lights, is a 1949 Leyland Titan PD2/1 with a Brush body; it is working on the 35 route, which ran an express limited stop service to the Maypole over the tram route. *F. N. Lloyd Jones*

Bottom Unlike in neighbouring Edgbaston, land in Balsall Heath was sold off in a far more piecemeal fashion and when, in 1833, the Rev Vincent Edwards died, it was a golden opportunity for Balsall Heath to develop rapidly. By 1862, the year that it obtained Urban District status, the previously rural area had become

an urban suburb with a population of 10,000 crammed into some 10 miles of streets. In the next 30 years, Balsall Heath became a 'honey-pot' of industrial development and had its own School Board, hospital, and water and sewage management schemes. Yet in 1891 it was annexed by its big brother, much to the chagrin of the local population, of whom only 10% bothered to vote! Soon afterwards, in 1896, a Free Library was opened in Moseley Road, unusually combined with an Art Nouveau-fronted swimming baths, though the latter was not opened until 1907 as the water was to be supplied from an artesian well – this seemed like a good idea until the water-bearing rocks were reached at a depth of 727 feet! The Free Library is housed in the building on the left with three decorative gables, while the baths are next to the little cart parked beneath the trees. On the right is the Moseley Road Art School, opened in 1900. The tram travelling into Birmingham is car 43, one of the 35hp Brill 21E-trucked open-top trams that entered service in June 1906 and was drafted to the newly opened Moseley Road depot to replace the CBT steam trams on 1 January 1907. *Author's collection*

Above right Cars 431 and 435 pass Horrell & Bowman's Triplex depot at No 514 Moseley Road in July 1949, the two open-balcony cars showing clearly the difference between the pre-war and post-war liveries. Two children lean on the wrought-iron rails of the open balcony on this sunny afternoon, oblivious to the impending closure of the tram route and the end of their exhilarating, windy tram rides. One

wonders how many of the 50-plus passengers on the leading tram are looking at the Imperial Cinema (whose canopy is just visible on the extreme right of the picture) and considering whether to go and see Alan Ladd and Robert Preston in *Whispering Smith*. The Imperial Picture Palace opened on 26 January 1914 and finally closed in 1983. During the night of 25 October 1940, during the showing of an earlier film starring Robert Preston with Dorothy Lamour, somewhat inappropriately titled *Typhoon*, a bomb dropped through the nearby Carlton Cinema and exploded in front of the screen; 19 people died, many of whom were still sitting upright in their seats, unmarked, but dead. The blast had burst their lungs! Opposite the cinema is Edward Road, which provided access to the 37 and 39 routes from the depot (see pages 98-9). The area between Edward Road and Balsall Heath Road was nicknamed 'bomb alley' during the war because of the amount of high explosives dropped on it between autumn 1940 and spring 1941. *R. Brook*

Above With the Brighton Road traffic lights on red, car 337, on the 48 route, waits at the head of a queue of cyclists, a Morris 10 and an Austin 16hp. This section of Moseley Road became important, with its baths, library, Friends' Institute, Art School and numerous churches, as the centre of the briefly independent Balsall Heath between 1862 and 1891. Prior to its annexation by Birmingham, the council, or Local Board as it was known, built up the infrastructure of the area, much of which remains today. UEC open-balcony car 337 was only drafted into Moseley Road's allocation of trams from Washwood Heath depot five weeks before the abandonment. It was the last tram to work on the 39 route from Hill Street to Alcester Lanes End via Balsall Heath on 1 October 1949. *R. T. Wilson*

Moseley Road Depot, Kings Heath and Alcester Lanes End

Above Looking southwards along Moseley Road from the Brighton Road traffic lights towards Moseley Road depot, obscured by distant car 429, we can see the climb towards Park Road where the 39 route from Balsall Heath joined the main route. Car 429 is working inbound from Kings Heath via Leopold Street to the Hill Street terminus, and is being followed by 435, again working into the city but on the 42 route to Albert Street; the latter car is opposite the entrance to Moseley Road depot. The land behind the trees to the right was used for overnight parking of buses by Birmingham City Transport pending the conversion of the depot to bus operation. In the far distance is a Daimler COG5 working towards the city on the 35 route. *R. T. Wilson*

Below Grey-painted, four-wheel tram 345 stands in the dark recesses of Moseley Road depot early in October 1947 in store and awaiting scrapping, after having been the penultimate tram on the Ladywood 33 route on the night of Saturday 30 August 1947. It would remain in this state until January 1948 when it was finally broken up by George Cohen & Son Ltd. Of the 50 cars of the 301 Class painted in wartime grey, 345 was one of only five not to revert to the standard blue and cream livery. To the left is car 449, only the third member of the 401 Class to be withdrawn. It would languish even longer in the depot before finally being scrapped on 12 November 1949. A massive sort-out of some 25 withdrawn four-wheelers took place between October 1948 and January 1949. On the extreme left is van 5, built at Kyotts Lake Road Works in 1913; mounted on a Brill 21E truck, it was used for most of its career as a sand van, before being broken up in August 1949. The pre-war-liveried tram behind it appears to be car 566, which was at Moseley Road for electrical re-cabling. The totally enclosed bogie car on the right is car 531, which was also being re-cabled at the depot. *F. N. Lloyd Jones*

On Friday 26 August 1949 one of the UEC-built air and oil brake cars, 422, still in its pre-war livery, stands outside the imposing frontage of the depot. Situated just beyond Brighton Road, it had two entrances from Moseley Road on either side of the office buildings; a set of tracks can be seen just beneath 422, and the second set in front of car 339. This latter car had been drafted in from Miller Street to cover a shortage of trams and, despite its post-war livery, was due to be withdrawn when the Moseley Road routes closed on Saturday 1 October 1949. Unlike UEC-bodied four-wheeler 339, which had at least 17 changes of depot and operated all over the city, the 401-450 Class spent virtually all their working life at Moseley Road; car 422 was one of the final 38 of the class to operate the last narrow-gauge, open-balcony, regular all-day service in Britain.

Seen between the two trams is the Moseley & Balsall Heath Institute. Built in 1883 and designed in a pseudo-ecclesiastical Gothic style by a local builder, John Bowen, it was to become the cultural focus of the Balsall Heath area. One night in October 1940, when a jazz band was playing there, a bomb went straight through the roof of the depot next door and through one end of car 514. Fortunately it did not explode, otherwise a certain tramway photographer who was the tenor saxophonist that night would not have been able to take some of the

photographs that appear in this and the companion volumes.

In almost the same position as car 422 in the previous photograph, a Travel West Midlands Volvo B7L with an Alexander H47/27F body, 4259 (BU51 RVT), which entered service in December 2001, heads past the frontage of the old Moseley Road tram depot and subsequent bus garage. It closed on 15 February 1975 and after much varied use, including a go-karting arena and track and a skate-board centre, some 29 years later it is having some restoration work undertaken on its Grade II listed frontage. Bus 4259 is working on the 50 route along Moseley Road on 15 January 2002, heading for the Druids Heath housing development. *T. J. Edgington/D. R. Harvey*

Below With abandonment approaching, the 401 Class were not all repainted in the post-war livery, and the previous lined-out style with primrose rocker panels became increasingly weatherbeaten. Car 418, working the Alcester Lanes End service from Albert Street, climbs Moseley Road on 9 July 1949 at the Park Road junction, where Balsall Heath trams met the main Moseley Road route (see also page 100). The passengers on the open balcony get a little protection from the wing window opposite the stairhead, but by 1949 passengers on public transport were expecting something a little better. Despite being fitted with transverse cushioned seats in the lower saloon, these trams belonged to the pre-First World War level of technology. Lack of investment in the tramway system from the mid-1930s gradually introduced the idea among the Transport Committee and Birmingham's public that the trams were an anachronism. Of course, with no new stock after 1930 this became increasingly true and furthered the ever more convincing argument for abandonment.

The new post-war generation of buses is exemplified by the Leyland Titan PD2/1 bodied by Brush, which is following the tram on the 35 bus route to the Maypole terminus. This particular bus was the first of the class, numbered 1656 (HOV 656), and can easily be recognised as, for its first year or so in service, it carried its numberplate on the radiator, before it was moved to the more orthodox cab dash. These buses were splendid vehicles and pointed towards the more comfortable mode of transport that would replace the trams. The new bus services would be numbered 48, 49 and 50, thus replacing the 13 tram services and bus route 35 that plied along Moseley Road. It would, however, be of little comfort to the windswept balcony passengers on tram 418 to know that 1656, in common with all Birmingham's half-cab double-deckers, would not be fitted with heaters! *T. J. Edgington*

Bottom On Monday 26 September 1949 car 427 approaches the junction with Park Road as it travels towards the city on the 42 route. It is passing the splendidly styled 1930s petrol pumps, dispensing the present-day well-known brands of Shell and Esso and the long-forgotten Cleveland brand. In the background, bogie car 728 is waiting at Park Road, about half-way between Moseley Road depot and Moseley village. Park Road had originally been used by the Balsall Heath steam tram route into the city from 1884 until its abandonment on the last day of 1906 (see page 100). The same route was used by Birmingham Corporation, but when the electric tram route was closed, just five days after this photograph was taken, the replacement bus services did not use Park Road, which resumed its original role as a thoroughfare of lesser importance. *A. N. H. Glover*

Top Beyond Park Road the tram route negotiated two curves, then fell gently towards Moseley village. The Prince of Wales public house really marked the start of the shopping area at Moseley, and on a miserable day in 1949 car 445 has just passed the pub and is standing at the last request stop before St Mary's Row in the centre of the late-19th-century suburb. The tram is probably delaying the snub-nosed 1937 Fordson delivery van, while on the left the Coventry-registered Rover Twelve shows that the art of car parking and car abandonment was just as prevalent in 1949 as it is today! *F. N. Lloyd Jones*

Middle Moseley Road depot's allocation of trams had normally included not only the open-balconied four-wheelers of the 401 Class, but also a number of bogie cars. As many as 30 such totally enclosed tramcars had been allocated there before 1939, but over the next three years this was gradually reduced to none. However, from August 1947 the 11 cars of the 702 Class from the sequence 716 to 731 that survived the Second World War returned to Moseley Road. Car 717, one of these 1925 Brush-built, all-electric bogie cars, leaves St Mary's Row for the city on the 39 route. In early post-war days bogie cars were usually confined to the Balsall Heath service from Hill Street. The tram is carrying the advertisement for 'Tizer, The Appetizer', a drink that came in a peculiarly erotically shaped bottle. The prospect of purchasing a small bottle of Tizer always seemed to be reaching far more into the realms of the adult world than, say, a bottle of lemonade! *Lens of Sutton*

Bottom The steeply gabled Edwardian shops in Moseley village, where car 409 waits at the tram stop before travelling towards the city via Balsall Heath on the 39 route, have barely changed since 1949. This view of car 409 was taken at the same location as above, but from the other side of the road. The open-balconied tram is passing a large 1938 Walsall-registered Hillman six-cylinder saloon; before the Second World War Hillman manufactured large luxury cars, and this model was later developed as the Humber Snipe. Overtaking the somewhat down-at-heel tram with its weatherbeaten paintwork is a wartime Austin 30cwt van. This belonged

to a type that ranged from this, the smallest, up to 5-ton lorries, and, because they had the general appearance of one of their main competitors, they were known as 'Birmingham Bedfords'. *R. T. Wilson*

Top The Birmingham Central Tramways Company began operation of its steam trams to Moseley on 29 December 1884, with its original town terminus in Bradford Street. The Moseley terminus was just beyond the Fighting Cocks

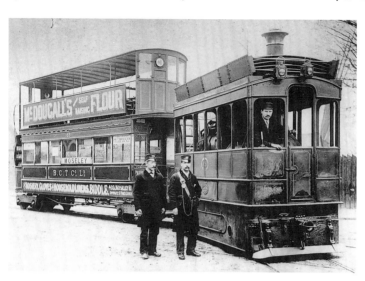

public house and the trams were able to run around the adjacent Moseley Village Green, at the bottom of St Mary's Row, which had been encircled with tram tracks. Within a few years a coke yard, with a servicing pit, ash pits and a fresh water supply, had been put into St Mary's Row and the turning loop became disused. BCT steam tram locomotive No 45, one of 14 built by the Falcon Engine Company in 1885, pulling double-ended 60-seat trailer 63, also built by Falcon but in the following year, stands in Moseley Road with the locomotive half turned into St May's Row in the early 1890s. The steam tram gained a poor reputation among Edwardian electric tram proponents, but when properly maintained 'the shufflers', so named because of their shuffling gait as the pistons pumped back and forth, were very efficient movers of people. The wooden fence in the background marks the boundary of the grounds of Moseley Hall, which would be given to the city by its owner, Richard Cadbury, in 1890 as a children's hospital; in 1899 its grounds would be cut in half by Salisbury Road, named after Queen Victoria's last Prime Minister; he held that office three times and died in 1903, just one year after the end of his last seven-year tenure. The open land behind the tram was used within a few years for the site of the distinctive gable-ended shops seen in the previous picture. *Author's collection*

Middle Still painted with a dark roof in 1949, a relic from the wartime blackout restrictions, Metro-Cammell-bodied Daimler COG5 single-decker 57, AOP 57, waits for the traffic lights to change before negotiating the junction with Salisbury Road in Moseley village. This 1935-built bus – used throughout the war as an ambulance – is running empty to take up service in the city, hence the destination display. Tram 426 is really working on the 42 route, but the unusual destination number 67 was put up for the benefit of the photographer. Salisbury Road is to the right. *W. A. Camwell, courtesy of P. Jaques*

Bottom Car 421 was one of the 50 UEC-bodied open-balcony cars

introduced between August 1912 and March 1913 and fitted with Mountain & Gibson 7ft 6in trucks and Dick, Kerr DK19A 40hp motors. Although earmarked for the new Spencer-Dawson air and oil brake, they were placed in service over the BCT system as the need demanded until the new brakes became available. Being low-height cars, at 15ft 7½in, they could pass beneath Aston station and Selly Oak railway bridges. Once fitted with the air and oil brake, which failed with the brakes locked on, all the class were allocated to Moseley Road depot and were then allowed to work on the 1 in 13 hill in Leopold Street on the 40 and 41 routes (see page 89). As car 421 is fitted with flop-over boards

showing the destination, and has the route identification letter 'M', this photograph must have been taken by 1915, when the letter system fell into disuse. In fact, car 421 is working the steep Leopold Street route where its oil and air brake would be employed. The tower on the right belongs to the splendid terracotta-detailed Fighting Cocks pub built in 1899 at a cost of £4,000 by the Holt Brewery Company, together with the shops in St Mary's Row, also to the right; they were built in a vaguely Dutch style, and have a certain architectural panache about them, unlike the steeply gabled shops opposite. *Commercial postcard*

Top The first member of the UEC-built four-wheelers of 1913, car 401, leaves the Reddings Road stop when working the 42 route in the summer of 1949. It will go down the hill and past the police station on its way to Moseley village some quarter of a mile away. This tram stop not only served the large houses in the area, but also the Moseley Rugby Football Club, which for many years was Birmingham's premier team, and whose ground, The Reddings, was situated in Reddings Road. Alas, hard times, professional Rugby Union and legal problems led to the rapid decline of Moseley RFC and the site was sold for

housing in the late 1990s. The late, great Sam 'The Boot' Doble must be turning in his grave! *R. T. Wilson*

Above Once out of Moseley, Alcester Road climbed a steady gradient known as Welsh's Hill and passed the entrance to Moseley Hall, a Georgian house built by the Taylors, a banking family who formed a partnership that is still with us today in the form of Lloyds Bank. The hall was burned down in 1791 when anti-Republican fervour among a Tory-inspired drunken mob resulted in the so-called 'Church and King Riots' in which anyone with Republican sympathies was attacked. The hall was rebuilt in 1796, but by 1884 had been purchased by Richard Cadbury, the chocolate manufacturer. Two years later Cadbury moved to Uffculme House in Moor Green and donated Moseley Hall to Birmingham for use as a convalescent home. Once over the hill at Moor Green Lane, Alcester Road drops down to the junction with Queensbridge Road, where four-wheel car 438 is seen on 19 April 1947. It is travelling away from Moseley village, having passed Moseley Hall about 2 minutes earlier, and has just passed the junction across which a young, short-trousered cyclist pedals carefully over the tram tracks. *T. J. Edgington*

Above Just beyond Queensbridge Road is the bridge carrying High Street over the former Birmingham & Gloucester Railway, opened in 1840; it runs in a cutting behind the advertising hoardings above the Austin Ten that is turning into Valentine Road. A rather full tramcar, 420, is working on the 39 route to Alcester Lanes End via Balsall Heath in April 1947, and is about to stop opposite the entrance to Kings Heath station, although the tram is six years too late to connect with trains, the station having closed on 27 January 1941! With hindsight, Birmingham Corporation's advertising policy regularly produced peculiar juxtapositions of advertisements: car 420 is carrying 'Drink delicious Typhoo Tea, so very refreshing!', but also adverts for the laxative Ex-Lax as well as Beechams Pills, perhaps suggesting that concern with our digestive tracts is less today than it was then. *A. N. H. Glover collection*

Opposite below The village of Kings Heath, known as Kyngesheth in 1511, grew in a linear pattern in the mid-19th century along what was later to become known as High Street. It first became a separate parish on 13 January 1863, and was still part of Kings Norton UDC when the steam tram route was extended from Moseley village to the terminus at Institute Road on 1 February 1887. The High Street later became a major suburban shopping centre, as can be seen from the 1920s shops next to the tram, including a branch of the well-known grocery chain of George Mason. The Kings Heath & Moseley Institute, whose church-like tower can be seen behind the tram, was built in 1878, using money donated by philanthropist J. H. Nettlefold, whose family was part of the Guest, Keen & Nettlefold (later GKN) screw-manufacturing company. Car 725, which has just passed Institute Road, was one of 30 cars built by Brush in 1925, with EMB Burnley-type maximum-traction bogies and GEC WT32H 40hp motors. In their final years these bogie cars usually worked on the Cannon Hill and Alcester Lanes End via Balsall Heath services; here, in 1949, car 725 is working the 39 service, followed by car 423 on the 42 route. Members of the 702 Class spent most of their working lives before and after the Second World War operating from Moseley Road, but their brief sojourn at Miller Street and Witton in the early part of the war saw no fewer than nine of them destroyed at the latter depot. One more tram was destroyed in Miller Street in April 1941 and a further car was withdrawn as an accident victim. In addition to these, a further 11 trams, including 725, received some structural damage. *F. N. Lloyd Jones*

Top right The crosses on this postcard refer to a comment written on the back: 'under the third roof...uncle's shop'. Mr Gough's shop sold stationery and unusually had a lending library. So that's where this postcard came from! In this very early view of electric tramcar operation in Kings Heath's, car 173, one of the UEC-bodied tramcars of 1907 built with Mountain & Gibson 7ft 6in radial trucks, is working from Alcester Lanes End via Balsall Heath on the 'K' route through the busy High Street. The route letters were replaced by numbers in 1915 and flop-over boards replaced the canopy destination boxes; car 173 is carrying 'the full set', suggesting that it is about 1908. A second tramcar of the same batch, possibly car 185, is coming up High Street's hill towards All Saints Church and the junction with Vicarage Road on the left opposite Mr Gough's emporium. *Commercial postcard*

Above The spire of All Saints Church dominates the skyline at the far end of Kings Heath shopping centre. When this photograph was taken it was only some 15 years since it had been completed with the building of its south-west tower. Car 88, with flop-over destination boards and displaying the route letter 'M', stands at the top of High Street in about 1910. It was one of the Mountain & Gibson 8ft 6in radial-truck cars built by UEC between August 1906 and March 1907. Originally open-balcony and open-vestibule trams, all had their vestibules enclosed from 1923. These 52-seater trams were quite tall at 16ft 0½in, but could negotiate the Stratford Road and Coventry Road railway bridges. Car 88 would be replaced on the Moseley Road services by 1914 when the 401 Class took over the running of most of the services. The radial trucks under these trams were a source of trouble within a few months of entering service: after a tram turned a corner the axle on the truck did not return to the straight position. In an attempt to cure the problem the trucks were made rigid, but this was not a complete success. After 19 years of alterations and replacements, all the remaining radial trucks were replaced on the 71 Class, with no fewer than 135 trams, including car 88, being placed on Peckham P35 trucks. *Commercial postcard*

Above The wall to the right of tramcar 416 in this photograph, taken on Friday 2 September 1949, belongs to All Saints Church. Beyond is identical car 425, incidentally repainted in post-war livery with the simpler style of post-war fleet number, working on the 40 short-working to Kings Heath; it will take the cross-over to stand behind 416, which has also worked to this destination, but which will return to Hill Street via Leopold Street. The view out of the city south-westwards has changed out of all recognition. Car 425 is opposite the subterranean public lavatories that stood in the middle of Vicarage Road, and which were finally replaced in 1993. Also having disappeared over the intervening years are all the distant trees in the main Alcester Road South beyond All Saints Road, which were cut down in the 1960s when

an anonymous low-height concrete box structure of shops was built. Today the site of these shops is mainly occupied by a Sainsbury's supermarket. *T. J. Edgington*

Below Beyond Kings Heath the trams ran down to the Howard Road crossing before climbing a long gentle gradient to the Alcester Lanes End terminus. Car 414, working the 42 route, is approaching the junction from the Kings Heath direction early in 1949. Although the small terrace of houses has been demolished, this stretch of Alcester Road South is still recognisably the same, despite numerous plans to upgrade the road since the nearby M40/M42 was opened, which made parts of Birmingham including Kings Heath more accessible to car-borne commuters. *F. N. Lloyd Jones*

Top Looking out of Kings Heath across the junction with Howard Road, car 445 is seen working on the 42 route to Alcester Lanes End, having come from the city terminus in Albert Street. The road gently climbs through the tree-lined Alcester Road South, passing the junction with Wheelers Lane on the left, about a third of the way towards the distant terminus. Car 445, by now in its final post-war-style livery, appears to still have a good number of passengers, many of whom would have to face the long walk to the Maypole or catch the express service 35 bus; this had protective fares, but although it cost more than the tram, it was much quicker. *A. K. Terry*

Middle The last day of the Kings Heath tram routes was Saturday 1 October 1949. A normal service was maintained throughout the day, and in the evening the trams were used, as they had been for many years, to provide the service for a Kings Heath dog-track meeting at the racecourse just beyond the tram terminus. This line-up of trams, seen at about six o'clock that evening, is standing near the terminus, just north of the junction with Taylor Road. It is led by car 731, the last all-electric bogie car to enter service with Birmingham Corporation, some 24 years earlier. The intending spectators, leaving the trams for the last time, would be carried by brand-new Daimler CVD6 buses for the next meeting. Unusually, car 731 has worked the 42 route from Albert Street rather than the more normal 401 Class four-wheelers lined up behind it. In the distance is one of the 1948 batch of Leyland Titan PD2/1s, which, like 731, had Brush bodies. Kings Heath dog-track closed in March 1971 and its site is now a housing estate. *A. N. H. Glover*

Bottom On that final day, and looking in need of the repaint that it would never receive, car 447 stands at the same location near Taylor Road, where the 18 bus crossed Alcester Road South. Carrying the balcony dash advertisement for the Kings Heath ladies outfitter E. R. Green,

this tram, in company with the rest of the 401 Class that survived to the end of tramcar operation, will later be driven back to Moseley Road depot, where it will be broken up by George Cohen & Sons Ltd as one of the final nine cars of the class to be scrapped in December 1949.

These open-balcony cars ran on average some 858,000 miles in their 37 years of service; one wonders if a 1967-built double-decker bus would be welcomed as anything other than a museum piece if it turned up today on an all-day working on the Alcester Road routes. *A. N. H. Glover*

Below On Thursday 14 April 1939, the day that Adolf Hitler drove into Vienna, Brush totally enclosed car 714 stands at the Alcester Lanes End terminus at Kings Heath, preparing to work back to Hill Street via Balsall Heath. The driver is passing a few moments with his conductor before clocking in at the Bundy clock, just behind the bread van. This tram was unfortunate as it became the first bogie car to be taken out of service. It overturned, after a combination of a faulty controller and failure by the motorman to obey braking regulations, at the bottom of the long hill on the corner of Park Road and Witton Lane in March 1940. The top deck was badly damaged and, after being stored throughout the war in Sampson Road paint shop, it was broken up by August 1945. *H. B. Priestley*

Bottom At 11.05am on Sunday 23 January 1949, car 407 waits for further passengers at the Alcester Lanes End terminus. It is standing outside the Kings Arms public house before taking the main Moseley Road route into the city centre. Exactly one month later, on 24 February, car 407 was repainted, presumably at considerable expense, in the post-war livery with plain fleet numbers, despite being scheduled for withdrawal in October 1948! Because of the Second World War, these trams remained in service well beyond their expected lifespan. However, they did have the advantage of having the air and oil brake, which allowed them to run over all Moseley Road depot's routes. As long as there were insufficient bogie cars and the Moseley Road group of services were kept running, the 401 Class was safe. Nine months later the routes had closed, the 401s were being broken up by George Cohen & Sons in the depot, their home for 37 years, and all the totally enclosed allocation of 702 Class bogie cars had been transferred to Miller Street.

The side window destination blind for this route reads 'ALCESTER LANES END AND DALE END', when in fact the terminus was in Albert Street; Dale End had been used from 1921 to 1930, when the central island in this wide street had on it an elaborately decorated cast-iron, glass-roofed shelter. The Alcester Lanes End trams, together with those that traversed Coventry Road, Stratford Road and Warwick Road, all terminated there; however, although the 42, 48, 50 and 65 routes

moved into Albert Street, some trams still retained this rather confusing destination display as their linen blinds were virtually indestructible. *A. N. H. Glover*

Above The use of the 71 Class of Mountain & Gibson radial truck tramcars, built in 1906 with UEC bodies, on the Moseley Road services virtually ended when the 50 four-wheelers of the 401 Class retrospectively fitted with the Spencer-Dawson air and oil brake arrived at Moseley Road depot in the latter half of 1913. Car 108, without vestibule screens and still using flop-over destination boards, stands at the terminus at Alcester Lanes End outside 'the Knob', the local name for the Kings Arms. The crossroads, with Woodthorpe Road on the right and Taylor Road on the left, was, during the early 19th century, the site of a toll-house; with traffic having to slow down to pay the toll, entrepreneurs set up a hostelry and a few places to buy food, and the equivalent of the modern motorway service station was in place. When tram 108 was pictured in about 1910, the area had become a suburb of Birmingham, although it would be another 50 years before serious urban development would build over the farmland out to the city boundary at the Maypole. *Author's collection*

Right Looking remarkably spick-and-span, UEC-built car 428 stands at the Alcester Lanes End terminus equipped with white-painted fenders and with its headlight masked. Above the tramcar, underneath the bracket arm, is a trolley-finder; these were used during the war at places such as termini where trolleypoles would have to be turned, helping the conductor to guide the pole to the wire and avoiding any flashes in the blackout conditions. Southwards away from the city was Kings Heath dog-track, which remained open throughout the hostilities. Beyond that, Alcester Road South was being developed as far as the city boundary at the

Maypole, with the inter-war semi-detached houses being separated from the road by wide grass verges. The meandering, single-carriageway road is still waiting, more than 60 years later, for this congested main route to be made into a straighter dual-carriageway, although this may now never happen. *R. T. Wilson*

INDEX OF LOCATIONS